BEING A SUPER
TRANS ALLY!

of related interest

Becoming an Ally to the Gender-Expansive Child
A Guide for Parents and Carers
Anna Bianchi
ISBN 978 1 78592 051 6
eISBN 978 1 78450 305 5

Phoenix Goes to School
A Story to Support Transgender and Gender Diverse Children
Michelle and Phoenix Finch
Illustrated by Sharon Davey
ISBN 978 1 78592 821 5
eISBN 978 1 78450 924 8

Are You a Boy or Are You a Girl?
Sarah Savage and Fox Fisher
Illustrated by Fox Fisher
ISBN 978 1 78592 267 1
eISBN 978 1 78450 556 1

Trans Teen Survival Guide
Owl and Fox Fisher
ISBN 978 1 78592 341 8
eISBN 978 1 78450 662 9

Everything You Ever Wanted to Know about Trans (But Were Afraid to Ask)
Brynn Tannehill
ISBN 978 1 78592 826 0
eISBN 978 1 78450 956 9

BEING A SUPER TRANS ALLY!

A Creative Workbook and Journal for Young People

Phoenix Schneider, MSW and Sherry Paris, MEd

Illustrated by Sherry Paris

Jessica Kingsley Publishers
London and Philadelphia

Though this work may provide general guidance associated with the subject matter contained herein, it is not intended to prescribe or recommend any specific course of action associated with actual events or situations. Illustrations, names, characters, places, and events described in this book are either the products of the authors' imagination or used in a fictitious manner. Any resemblance to actual persons, living or dead, or actual events is purely coincidental.

First published in 2020
by Jessica Kingsley Publishers
73 Collier Street
London N1 9BE, UK
and
400 Market Street, Suite 400
Philadelphia, PA 19106, USA

www.jkp.com

Library of Congress Cataloging in Publication Data
A CIP catalog record for this book is available from the Library of Congress

British Library Cataloguing in Publication Data
A CIP catalogue record for this book is available from the British Library

ISBN 978 1 78775 198 9
eISBN 978 1 78775 199 6

Printed and bound in the United States

Dedications and Gratitude

Phoenix dedicates this book to his dad, David Schneider, who was his #1 fan and encouraged him to go to social work school to be the change he wished to see in the world. Phoenix hopes he is smiling proud, watching him fly; to his mom, Beverly Schneider, for her continued unconditional love and support since Phoenix came out as being trans. She loves to march alongside Phoenix in the Pride Parade as a proud mom and Super Trans Ally; to his partner and soul-unicorn, Jess Moore, whose love and encouragement mean the world to him; and to all the courageous, inspiring, and beautiful trans, non-binary, gender diverse, and gender-fabulous young people who inspire so many to be exactly who they are.

Sherry dedicates this book to her father, David Paris, for being her #1 cheerleader and a role model as a lifelong learner and an accepting, supportive person. Sherry is grateful beyond words for the abundant support and encouragement from her devoted spouse, Mel Tirado. Sherry thanks her beloved mother, Elaine Paris, for her timeless creativity and inspiration. Sherry drew the illustrations for this book using her mother's antique dip pens. This is her first endeavor as an illustrator.

Phoenix and Sherry are grateful to Jessica Kingsley Publishers for the opportunity to create this exciting book. We value the trust and support of Andrew James, Editorial Director, Simeon Hance, Editorial Assistant, Hannah Snetsinger, Production Editor, and Katherine Laidler, Copy Editor. Gratitude goes out to our youth and young people's advisory council: Helen Everbach, Soul Cooke, and Izzy Moore for their time, energy, and expertise in reviewing the draft text.

Contents

Introduction   **11**

Why are you needed as a Super Trans Ally?   11

What is your motivation for being a Super Trans Ally?   15

Write your Super Trans Ally mission statement   16

The difference between tolerance and acceptance   17

Super Trans Ally crossword puzzle of important terms   20

Fill in the blanks with the terms from the crossword puzzle   22

**Ch 1: Gender Is a Spectrum Beyond
a Binary and into Outer Space!**   **25**

Gender identity and gender expression multiple choice   26

Match the terms   30

Alphabet soup!   32

Gender diverse universe   35

Ch 2: Everyone Is a Unique Universe   **37**

Personal identities and traits   38

Draw yourself!   46

Guess which gender advertising would be directed towards   47

Gender binary impact checklist   48

Why are some people upset by gender diversity?   50

The gender universe   51

My gender experiences checklist   53

Journal prompt: How do you like to express your gender?   54

Yes, no, or maybe so? What do you think about gender?   55

Let's dance!   57

Ch 3: Your Loved One Is Trans and They Still Love the Same Colors!   **59**

Bubble gum: Connect   60

Erase-a-sketch-a-ssumptions away!   63

Bubble gum: Affirm   66

Ch 4: When We Say Everybody Is Included, We Mean Every BODY!   **69**

Identity: Fixed or fluid?   70

Judgmental questions   72

Coloring inside of the lines   73

Portraits of diverse trans and non-binary experiences   80

Re-do! Coloring outside of the lines   86

Transition and pronouns and names—Oh my!   92

OKTA (OK to ask) or NOYB (None of your business)   93

Pronoun practice makes perfect!   95

That's awkward! Situation responses   97

Things to do...do those things!   100

Snapshot of take-aways from this chapter   100

Ch 5: Ask, Don't Assume   **103**

Curiosity or interrogation?   104

Frequently asked questions about gender diverse friends and family   105

Responding to uncomfortable questions   105

Are you a good listener? 107

How do we create space for people to share their personal journeys with us? 109

Confidentiality quick quiz 111

Respectful boundaries scenario 113

Compliment or not? 114

Ch 6: Use Your Voice for Your Trans Sibling, Cousin, or Loved One and Help Grandma Remember 117

Who knows? 118

Assess what they know 119

Bubble gum: Support 120

Preparing yourself to talk to Grandma or your special relative 121

Role-play options for various possible scenarios
(supportive, questions/concerns, less supportive response) 123

"How should I react when I mess up?" Role-plays about
Grandma speaking to your gender diverse loved one 128

Debriefing with Grandma 131

Pronoun practice with Grandma! 132

Ch 7: Care Beyond a Pinky Swear 135

Ask–get–give 136

Too young? 137

From ageism to empowerment 141

Dismiss it (poetry/spoken word/songwriting) 144

Empathy and sympathy: What's the difference? 145

Sweat or sweet? 145

Do nothing/Say something/Go beyond 149

Bubble gum: Empower 155

Moving through frustration 155

Ch 8: Now You're the Teacher: School Everyone 157

Great educators 158

Bubble gum: Educate 162

En/Courage Zone 163

Questions about the en/courage zone   166

Speak up, interrupt, use humor, distract   168

Teaching your teachers: Cue scary music—dun dun dun!   172

Bubble gum: Take Action   178

Creating change at school   179

Letter writing   179

Self-check-in about letter writing   184

School visibility   185

Ch 9: Be a Super Trans Ally and Change the World!   187

Super Trans Ally checklist   188

Action items from the Super Trans Ally checklist   192

Template for planning an event for trans folks and allies   194

Recognizing my Super Trans Ally achievement(s)   195

What would be a fun way to reward or recognize yourself?   197

Gold star/share it forward   199

Inspired? Ready for action?   200

Chart to record your Super Trans Ally actions   202

Dreaming the world to come   204

Your vision for an inclusive world   205

Glossary of Terms   **209**

Resources   **217**

About the Authors   **221**

Introduction

Welcome! We are so excited that you are here! Thank you for trusting us to be part of your journey on the path as an ally to your friend(s) and/or family member(s) who identify as transgender, non-binary, gender expansive, gender fluid, genderqueer, Two Spirit, gender diverse, a different gender, or are questioning their gender. Everyone needs allies who offer support through challenges. Everyone can develop themself as an ally. We know that you have resources and compassion within you that will serve you well on this journey. Our hope is that through engaging with the activities in this book you will become an action-oriented Super Trans Ally. We hope you will find joy and excitement in this process. We'll be with you every step of the way.

WHY ARE YOU NEEDED AS A SUPER TRANS ALLY?

Can you see our open hearts and feel our arms outstretched to welcome you? We are educators and creators. We hold a vision for a world that is accepting of all genders. We work towards creating that world. We hope that you will help expand these energies. This book is a resource that you can use as a friendly guide in your efforts to reflect on yourself and others. We truly believe in you. We know that you have so much leadership potential. *"Who, me, a leader?"* Stay open to the possibilities! Maybe you are already an expert and a leader. Maybe you prefer to be behind the scenes. Remember, allies are needed at all levels in all capacities and in all ways. You may be the ally who quietly explains concepts or the ally who loudly proclaims it is time for change or the ally who writes letters or develops a game/app or starts a club or book group or holds a bake sale. Bring all of your skills and talents to the Super Trans Ally movement.

What if I don't know anyone who is trans or non-binary? Can I still read this book?
Absolutely! If you care about making your home, school, and community a safer and more accepting place for people of all genders, then this book is for you!

What if I am transgender, gender expansive, or identify as non-binary? Can I be a Super Trans Ally? Is this book for me?
Of course! People of all genders are encouraged to read this book and take ally action. You can be a Super Trans Ally!

I am in elementary school. Is this book for me?
Yes! Welcome! Thank you for your care and interest! This book has lots of activities that we hope you will find engaging. Please take time to use your creativity and color the pictures. Perhaps consider reading this book with a friend or loved one so you can discuss the ideas and ways to take action.

I am no longer considered a young person. Is it OK for me to enjoy the activities in this book?

Indeed! We hope that people of all ages will find this book filled with tools for your Super Trans Ally toolkit. It would be sweet to read this book as a family. Our hearts will be happy if teachers read this book with their classes. How about senior centers? What if Grandma brought this book to her book group? Then Grandma could be the one reminding other elders to use the correct pronouns! Increasing the level of healthy discussion about gender is important for people of all generations. This book is geared towards youth action and it can be useful to people of all ages and backgrounds. We encourage you to color the pictures, too!

What if I'm already an expert?

You will find activities and ideas in this book that help you expand your collection of Super Trans Ally tools.

My allyship is primarily for another issue. Will my skill set transfer directly?

All of your skills and life experiences are valued and valuable in this endeavor. Gender is a broad category and it intersects with every other identity category. Whatever your social justice passion might be, we stand with you. We stand for the dignity and full human rights of all people. We stand with you in creating a world in which we all get to be our authentic selves, stand in our truth, have the resources we need, and lead meaningful and connected lives free from unjust treatment in a sustainable environment on a planet we cherish. We are all in this together. We need all strategies and all people who care. We are glad you bring experience and skills to this journey.

Why is this book needed?

Trans and non-binary folks are a diverse group. We come in all different ages, shapes, and sizes. We are every race, ethnicity, nationality, religion, culture, ability/disability, social class, sexual orientation, mental health status, immigration status, relationship/family status, and every identity category. We are everywhere. We are stealth (flying under the radar), discrete, and out. Trans allies are also a diverse group. Together, we are a force for good. We stand together to affirm our self-determination and need for social change. Given our diversity, the needs of one person or community may be different from the needs of another person or community. We do not claim to know what is needed by all trans people in all communities. Ask questions. Don't assume.

Why are trans allies needed?

What is the difference between being a friend and being an ally? It's great to have a friend and to be a friend. We can never underestimate the power of and value of true friendship. An ally is someone who stands with us, speaks up on our behalf, and stands up for us. Friends and family members often act as our allies, but not always. Some friends are not comfortable speaking up. Allies are often our friends but not always. A random person in the hallway who interrupts a bullying situation is an ally even though we may not know them (yet!). Imagine two overlapping circles. The first circle represents people who are friends. The second circle represents people who are allies. The overlapping area is for those people who are both friends and allies. If you have a trans or non-binary friend or family member, it is wonderful to maintain that close relationship. We hope that you will also take steps to actively make the world a better place. That is what will make you a Super Trans Ally!

We honor, remember, and recognize those who have been doing this work for years, decades, and generations. Does it seem as if transgender folks are being featured more often or trans issues are more prevalent now? Do transgender rights seem like a new issue? Transgender and non-binary people have always existed, and activists have been working continuously towards creating a safer and more accepting society. There is an increase in public awareness of the concerns and rights of gender diverse people. There is also a deeply concerning increase in laws aimed at restricting the rights of transgender people and continued alarming rates of interpersonal violence and self-harm.

Transgender individuals and communities experience higher-than-average levels of bullying, harassment, violence, and mental health issues. There is a need for family and friends to take a strong stand to help challenge and change harmful transphobia, which is fear and hatred in the form of words and actions towards trans and non-binary people. Together, we can change the world. Supportive friends and family can create a buffer, a safe space to offer rest and comfort for the (sometimes weary) trans traveler.

As an ally to people of all genders, you are not in this alone. Your efforts are wanted, needed, and valued. We stand with you. We offer this book as a set of tools to help you empower yourself, to have fun, to help you overcome fears, recognize your strengths, develop your voice, and increase your willingness to take steps that make a difference.

WHAT IS YOUR MOTIVATION FOR BEING A SUPER TRANS ALLY?

Check all that apply:

☐ Love
☐ Frustration/anger

    ☐ Sadness
    ☐ Excitement to make a difference
    ☐ Fear for my loved one's life
    ☐ To change the world
    ☐ It's necessary and important
    ☐ Other: _____

WRITE YOUR SUPER TRANS ALLY MISSION STATEMENT

Why do you want to be a Super Trans Ally?
I want to be a Super Trans Ally to/because:

Remember to make your actions a collaboration whenever possible. Allies support; they don't take center stage. Yes, it's true that allies are featured as primary in this book. It's all ally all the time in our activities! We caution you to avoid the "diva ally" showcase! That show is not featured on the network!

Remember to do everything with love. Feel into your own heart and check to see if your motivation is love. Find ways to infuse love into your relationship with your gender diverse friends and family. Show your love through action as a Super Trans Ally. Even in challenging circumstances, hold on to that love as inspiration. Why do we want to make the world a more accepting and inclusive place?

Because we love our gender expansive friends and family members and want our efforts to help create a world in which we can all be ourselves without fear. We believe that the formula for social change is love + power + community action. Through individual and collective action, we are opening eyes, hearts, and minds to social justice for gender diverse people.

THE DIFFERENCE BETWEEN TOLERANCE AND ACCEPTANCE

What does it mean to tolerate something? It sounds like an uncomfortable situation! We tolerate mosquito bites because we know they are inevitable. We tolerate things we must endure because we don't have much of a choice. What does it mean to accept? Acceptance is a process of recognizing, acknowledging, understanding, and allowing. Acceptance flows best with lifelong learning and goes beyond awareness. Just because you are aware of something (like mosquito bites) does not mean that you accept them. What is the difference between tolerance and acceptance? Tolerance is obviously preferable to intolerance (bigotry) and yet it pales in comparison with acceptance. Let's imagine tolerance as a color; maybe it would be beige or grey. Acceptance, on the other hand, would be a rainbow with many facets and different ways of seeing those aspects. In your efforts to help educate others, remember the acceptance rainbow! Encourage others to go beyond tolerance towards full acceptance and inclusion of our transgender, non-binary, gender fluid, genderqueer, Two Spirit, and gender expansive friends and family.

A few immediate ways to demonstrate acceptance are by questioning our assumptions, evolving the ways we think, and using language thoughtfully. A thread throughout this book is the idea of erasing assumptions and the idea of not making assumptions. As humans, we can evolve the way we think about things. We also make mistakes and learn from them. We are all teachers and learners. This book offers creative activities to help you practice expanding your thinking, seeing things from different perspectives, and taking action.

Language is so important. Throughout this book we offer a variety of words to represent different gender identities. We hope that you will see yourself and your friends, family, and loved ones in this language. We use the pronoun "they" frequently. Some people question the legitimacy of this grammatically. English is a living and evolving language. "They" is now included in the dictionary as a singular pronoun (not just plural). If it sounds unfamiliar or un-comfortable to your ear, just be patient. It will become more familiar. Similarly, we may need to find new language for our relationships. A person whom you may previously have called a brother or sister may now prefer to be called a sibling. That may take some practice. A boyfriend or girlfriend may want to be called a partner. A mother or father may prefer to be called a parent. A husband or wife could now be referred to as a spouse. We explore language thoughtfully throughout the book. The language people use to describe gender and relationships will continue to evolve. We have used the language that is current at the time of publication. If any of the language does not suit you or the current trends, please change it! Literally, cross out whatever you would like and write in what makes sense now.

Key ideas in this book will be referred to as bubble gum. We want you to chew on these big ideas and make them stick! The bubble gum themes for Super Trans Allies are: Connect, Affirm, Support, Empower, Educate, and Take Action. Are you already chewing this yummy gum? Which new flavors would you like to enjoy? We will explore each of the bubble gum themes together.

We invite you to engage with this book in an active way. There are activities to help practice with language, including a crossword puzzle, fill-in-the-blanks, quizzes, and role-plays. You will have a chance to envision a new world and draw, collage, or write about your ideas. There are opportunities to write poems, stories, letters, and songs, and to journal. Chapter 2 invites you to explore your own identity categories. Have fun with all of it! Affirm yourself and create new understandings through engaging with the prompts. Put on your favorite music and dance as you strategize about actions you can take as a Super Trans Ally in Chapters 7, 8, and 9. Track your actions and reward yourself with the chart in Chapter 9.

Thank you for all that you already do and all that you intend to do to be a Super Trans Ally. We believe in you! We are excited to give you your Super Trans Ally cape! Here it is! Enjoy! It even comes with a tiny cape-carrying case that fits in your pocket!

SUPER TRANS ALLY CROSSWORD PUZZLE OF IMPORTANT TERMS

Throughout this book, there will be some language that is familiar to you and some that may be new to you. Please refer to the glossary as needed. Since there are endless possibilities for how a person may identify and experience their gender and the other parts of their identity, there is always room for learning even more about our diverse communities! Please keep in mind that these are very broad and general definitions for terms that have very personal meanings to different people. There is not just one way to define or experience any of these terms. Our identities are unique to us and the only one who can share what it means personally is *you*. The Super Trans Ally crossword puzzle on the next page will be a great guide to refer back to on this fabulous journey you are on! Please find the crossword puzzle's answers at the end of this chapter.

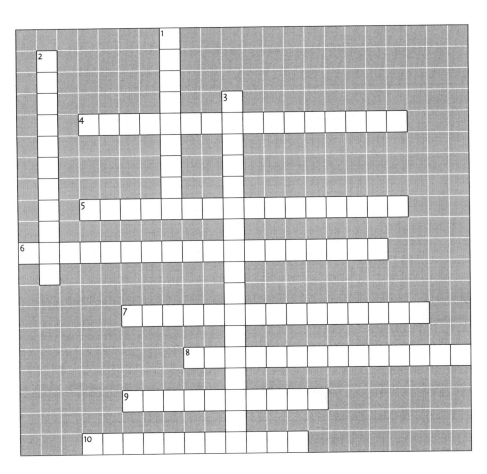

gender expression   gender expansive   genderqueer   transgender

sexual orientation   Super Trans Ally   cisgender   gender identity

non-binary   discrimination

ACROSS

4. Includes trans and non-binary identities; all whose gender challenges societal expectations about gender

5. A person who goes beyond being supportive to advocate with and for trans, non-binary, and gender diverse people/communities

6. A person's physical, sexual, romantic, emotional, spiritual attraction to a person of the same or different gender(s)

7. Personal internal knowledge of yourself as a woman, man, both, neither, or another gender

8. Words or actions towards a person of a specific community to cause harm to them

9. Beyond a gender binary of being exclusively male/boy or female/girl; not cisgender

10. A person whose gender is different from the one they were assigned/thought to be when they were born

DOWN

1. Gender a person was assigned/thought to be when they were born is the same as their gender now

2. A mix of male and female or neither; gender may be fluid

3. How a person walks, talks, dresses, plays; roles

Note: Spaces between words are included in the grid.

Created using the Crossword Maker on The TeachersCorner.net

FILL IN THE BLANKS WITH THE TERMS FROM THE CROSSWORD PUZZLE

If you are completing this activity with a group, create a short story or a group poem and use all of the terms or as many as you possibly can.

Complete the sentence

Use the words in the list below to complete the sentences.

sexual orientation	Super Trans Ally
gender expression	gender expansive
non-binary	genderqueer
discrimination	gender identity
transgender	cisgender

1. My friend Kai told me that they don't really feel like either a boy or a girl. They told me to use they/them as their pronouns and that they identify as

    _____.

2. Our friend Dalia is starting a petition to get an all-gender restroom at our school. She's a _____ because she is always advocating for the rights of trans people.

3. My sibling Trey has always felt like a different gender than the one she was thought to be when she was born. Our parents tried to raise her as a boy but it never felt right to Trey. I support and love my _____ sister!

4. The school decided that it was _____ to not allow trans students to use the locker room that

aligns with their gender identity. All students get to use the bathroom and locker room that affirms their gender.

5. I recently told my mom when she asked me if I like boys or girls that I like both and am attracted to people of all genders. I told her that my _____ is pansexual.

6. I like to tell people I am a _____ woman rather than just a woman because it's respectful to trans women and doesn't make them feel like an "other." We are both equally women.

7. It would be so much more inclusive if doctor's office forms would include a blank space for _____ rather than just male or female options.

8. My best friend Coco likes to wear a dress and have a mustache at the same time. Coco sometimes feels more feminine and sometimes feels more masculine. Coco is _____ and has a fluid gender.

9. My cousin Sam is a girl and really good at sports. She also has shorter hair and prefers to shop in the "boys" clothing stores and sections. She doesn't identify as a boy or trans. Her choices in how she likes to look, dress, and play are part of her _____ and how she feels most comfortable expressing herself.

10. At my camp everyone is welcome. They make sure that trans, non-binary, and _____ kids feel included so everyone has a great experience!

> **Please note that the answers will follow immediately afterwards. Hey, no peeking!**

Answer Key

Some of the terms can be used in more than one of the sentences. Try again and this time match different terms to some of the other sentences!

1. non-binary
2. Super Trans Ally
3. transgender
4. discrimination
5. sexual orientation

6. cisgender
7. gender identity
8. genderqueer
9. gender expression
10. gender expansive

Crossword Puzzle Answer Key

Down: 1. genderqueer; 2. cisgender; 3. gender expression. Across: 4. gender expansive; 5. Super Trans Ally; 6. sexual orientation; 7. gender identity; 8. discrimination; 9. non-binary; 10. transgender.

CHAPTER 1

Gender Is a Spectrum Beyond a Binary and into Outer Space!

Before we are even born and can have an opportunity to express who we are to the world, there is a story being told about who we are and what our place is in society. From the time we are born, we are socialized to fit the story being told about us.

We all learn from a very young age how to express our needs, desires, and, at some point, who we are and how we see ourselves and relate to others in the world. Do we fit into any of the existing boxes that may help define and shape who we are? Do these pre-made boxes feel limiting? Do we meet society's expectations of who we should be and how we should act? Do we challenge those expectations just by being our authentic selves?

If we are told something over and over and for a long period of time, it becomes ingrained and wired into our brains. It is how we are able to look at something, register it, and label it so quickly. We see something, we label it. We hear something, we label it. We label things using all of our senses. What happens when we see or hear something we've never seen or heard before? How do we process that new information and make sense of it? As children, we absorb things very quickly. In your experience as a young person, did you usually believe what you heard and learned from someone you trusted, such as a parent, teacher, relative, or friend? Did you also believe messages from strangers, acquaintances, television, movies, music, and social media? We tend to question what is true when we are given mixed messages from any of these sources. For adults who have been exposed repeatedly to social norms, the process of un-learning and accepting new information may be more complex. It often requires a mind up-grade, reboot, or complete rewiring of the brain when it comes to how we perceive, interpret, understand, and accept new information.

Now, let's talk about how this all relates to gender identity and expression. First, here is a short multiple-choice quiz to test your knowledge. Don't worry, it's not being graded!

GENDER IDENTITY AND GENDER EXPRESSION MULTIPLE CHOICE
• •

1. What is one thing that people do not usually ask when they know someone is pregnant r expecting to welcome a child?
    a. Are you hoping for a boy or a girl?
    b. Do you have a name picked for him or her?
    c. Are you going to have a gender reveal party?
    d. Are you going to wait until your child tells you what gender they are?

2. How many genders are there?
    a. 2
    b. 3
    c. 6
    d. 10
    e. Infinite

3. Is a person's gender expression related to their gender identity?
   a. Always
   b. Never
   c. Sometimes

4. A gender identity does not really exist until it is recognized by society as a real gender.
   a. True
   b. False

5. Any person can create a new gender identity if they do not fit into an existing gender box.
   a. True
   b. False

6. It's up to trans people to educate the rest of the non-trans world on topics surrounding gender identity and expression.
   a. True
   b. False

7. Gender is:
   a. A spectrum
   b. Infinite
   c. Diverse and expansive
   d. Exactly how one self-defines it for themself
   e. All of the above

Please note that the answers will follow immediately afterwards. Hey, no peeking!

Now let's look at the answers to the multiple-choice questions:

1. d

These questions are very common for someone who reveals they are pregnant or expecting to welcome a child. Most people become curious about the baby's gender. It's been a part of the whole baby culture for decades. Some prospective parents are making the decision not to tell people the baby's gender and not to gender their baby and wait until their kid tells them what feels right to them.

2. e

There are unlimited possibilities for how a person may identify their gender. When someone doesn't fit into an existing gender box, they can create a new box or say no to labels!

3. c

Some people would say they are very intentional about the clothes they wear, the way they wear their hair, the way they walk and talk, and the roles they take on. They may say that their gender expression is connected to their gender identity. Others would say that their expression is not tied to their gender identity. They may even omit the word gender from expression because it is the way that they express themselves regardless of their gender.

4. b

All gender identities exist and are real if the person says so. Just because a particular gender is not recognized by all in society does not make it any less real.

5. a

Any person on the planet can create a new gender that does not already exist. We are always evolving and are never stuck in pre-existing boxes that do not fit!

6. b

No. While it's important to value the voices of those with lived experience, trans people need the super allies in the world to stand up, be a voice, a teacher, a support, an advocate, and a decent, respectful, compassionate human being. Give trans people a break from being a 24/7 on-call educator. Let them live their lives with all the many important pieces of their identities.

7. e
Gender is a spectrum beyond a binary and into outer space!

Now, let's go on a sex and gender journey, starting with when we are born. Sex and gender are different. The sex assigned to us when we are born is usually determined by a doctor. It's based on our hormones, chromosomes, and genitalia. We have no say, even if we are crying to the doctor and parent(s) to let them know that they are way wrong. The gender we are thought to be when we are born is also what was assigned to us at birth without our consent. Male = boy. Female = girl. Intersex, when a baby's genitalia are not clearly aligned with the gender binary expectations, is also usually assigned as either a boy or a girl.

Gender is really just a bunch of expectations for girls/women and boys/men for how they are supposed to look, walk, talk, act, and be. Aren't there enough rules in our society? Gender rules are so limiting. Girls get pink. Boys get blue. Gendered colors = gender boring. When will society as a whole embrace the gender revolution that is inevitably happening? At a young age, we start to get mixed messages about gender and what it means. In some places and with some people, we can be boys who proudly wear pink or we can be girls who play football. We can use our chosen names and our pronouns in some spaces, but not everywhere. A chosen name is one that a person selects that feels more in alignment for them than their given/birth name. Some trans people refer to their name assigned at birth as their "dead name" and would rather not ever have to share it, or even think about it, ever again. With one group we are told that we are bold and beautiful, and with another group we are given the message that we are weak and invisible. It really can mess with the mind! We barely have time to live one life to its fullest, let alone a double or triple life where we can only be our true selves one-third of the time. Can you imagine how that might feel? Is that something that you have ever experienced? How can you can be a Super Trans Ally and make life a little easier for your trans, non-binary, and gender diverse friends and loved ones?

MATCH THE TERMS

Start by becoming as familiar as you possibly can with terminology related to gender and trans experience. Match the terms to the left with the descriptions on the right. An answer key follows the activity.

1. Toys

a. A range of negative attitudes, feelings, or actions towards trans people

2. Gender

b. When someone is referred to by the incorrect pronouns or gendered language (e.g. sir or miss)

3. Racism

c. A range of negative attitudes and discrimination towards people who are not straight

4. Transphobia

d. An assumption that a person's gender assigned at birth matches their gender identity

5. Restricted

e. A social construct and a set of societal expectations for what is appropriate and acceptable for boys/men and girls/women

6. Gender Binary

f. A right or advantage available only to a specific set of people

7. Homophobia

g. Associating something with a particular gender based on assumptions or stereotypes about gender expectations and roles

8. Sexism

h. Being limited in choices, for example: having only two gender options on applications and identity documents; having limited access to restrooms, locker rooms, and sports teams that align with one's gender.

9. Privilege

i. Often gendered but all of them are for every gender to play with

10. Misgender

j. Unfair treatment and stereotypes based on the social construct of race aimed at maintaining the social, political, and economic power of white people

11. Gendering

k. Unfair treatment and stereotypes targeting girls, women, femmes, and femininity with the conscious or unconscious aim of maintaining the social, political, and economic power of cisgender men

12. Cis-normativity

l. The assumption that there are only two genders, male and female

Please note that the answers will follow immediately afterwards. Hey, no peeking!

1. i	5. h	9. f
2. e	6. l	10. b
3. j	7. c	11. g
4. a	8. k	12. d

Can we stay on the ally action journey even when challenges arise? Can we interrupt, unlearn, and change systems which do not serve us well? Pay attention to the ways that racism shows up. Continue noticing the effects of sexism. Keep recognizing the symptoms of homophobia. What are the signs of classism, ableism, saneism, ageism? How do each of these social ills intersect with each other to cause increased harm to people who hold multiple identities? Ally action is essential in all areas. We feature transgender allyship in this book and urge you to take action in ways that consider the complicated set of social systems and often harmful effects of those systems. Take the broad view and the long view.

ALPHABET SOUP!

We are getting great practice with all of these terms and concepts and perhaps you are already an expert! Let's challenge ourselves to list as many words as we can think of related to gender and sexuality that begin with each of the letters of the alphabet. If you can think of multiple words that begin with the same letter, include them all! If you would have fun making this a speed challenge, give yourself five minutes to make the list. If you'd like a hint, think about the letters LGBTQ+ as a start. Ready, set, GO!

A. _____   B. _____

C. _____   D. _____

E. _____   F. _____

G. _____   H. _____

I. _____   J. _____

K. _____   L. _____

M. _____   N. _____

O. _____   P. _____

Q. _____   R. _____

S. _____   T. _____

U. _____   V. _____

W. _____   X. _____

Y. _____   Z. _____

Wow! There are so many terms and concepts related to gender and sexual orientation! For the rest of the book, we will use LGBTQIAPNBGD+ as shorthand to represent the vast diversity of human gender and sexuality. (See the glossary for definitions.)

> **Please note that the answers will follow immediately afterwards. Hey, no peeking!**

Partial answer key (since you will add to it!)

A. agender, allosexual, androgyne, androsexual, aromantic, asexual
B. bigender, bisexual
C. ceterosexual, cisgender
D. demiromantic, demisexual
E. _____

F. femme, finsexual

G. gay, gender diverse, gender expansive, gender fluid, gender nonconforming, genderqueer, grey-romantic, gynosexual

H. _____

I. Intersex

J. _____

K. _____

L. lesbian

M. _____

N. non-binary

O. _____

P. panromantic, pansexual, polygender, pomosexual

Q. queer, questioning

R. _____

S. Sapiosexual, skoliosexual

T. third gender, transgender, Two Spirit

U. _____

V. _____

W. _____

X. _____

Y. _____

Z. _____

Take Super Trans Ally ACTION. Love yourself. Live your truth. Accept others.

Rock it

GENDER DIVERSE UNIVERSE

Materials: paper (any kind), scissors, and any writing instrument (pen/pencil/marker/crayon).

Imagine that your mind is the caramel stretching when you bite into a chocolate caramel candy bar. You are the explorer. Visualize and feel your mind expanding as it travels beyond the binary and into the Gender Diverse Universe.

Draw an outline of planet Earth on one piece of paper (any size). Feel free to cut it out in the shape you want it to be in. What does gender look like on this planet? What words and images represent the different genders here? Draw and write down how gender is represented on Earth.

Questions:

1. Do people experience the gender binary as beneficial, neutral, harmful?

2. If so, what are the benefits and opportunities or risks and harms of having a binary system of gender? Consider the benefits and harms it can cause related to school, playgrounds, sports, activities, jobs, bathrooms, clothes, etc.

Now, expand beyond the binary and into outer space. Use your imagination. If there were human life on another planet, how would gender look there? Pick a new planet and draw its outline. How would you portray gender on this new planet using images and words?

Questions:

1. What were some of the **similarities** between the portrayals of gender on Earth and the other planet?

2. What were some of the **differences** between the portrayals of gender on Earth and the other planet?

Now come back to Earth. If you could have your ideal gender portrayal, how would you envision gender using images and language? Are there elements from the different planet you want to bring back to Earth? Does gender exist on your ideal planet? If it doesn't exist, how would that affect you personally? How would it affect society as a whole? What would gender look like, if anything, in your ideal world?

While our ideal vision for how gender would exist or not exist here on Earth may not be a reality at this time, we can continue to create and incorporate our ideal representation of gender into our own lives. We can live it and encourage others to live their most authentic selves!

CHAPTER 2

Everyone Is a Unique Universe

Understanding Gender and Self-Expression

Let's think about the vast array of personal identities and traits, and then we'll delve deeply into ideas about gender and self-expression.

Fill in the blanks below or circle your choices for your personal characteristics at this moment. Please refer to the glossary for general definitions. All terms are ultimately defined by your experience. Many categories are subject to change in the future! If the way that you think about yourself or your experience is not listed, please write it in.

If any of these categories are uncomfortable to write down or if you are not sure how to respond, feel free to leave the item blank. It's really OK. This is a tool for you. It will not be graded! Have fun with it. You may look back years from now and be curious about how things have changed over time.

For uncomfortable categories, do ask yourself why there is discomfort. Is it a personal issue, a social issue, fear of judgment or harm? Self-protection? Can you determine where the origin of the discomfort is in your personal experience? Was there an issue or incident? Please reach out to a trusted friend, family member, or professional for support if needed.

PERSONAL IDENTITIES AND TRAITS

• •

Today's date:

1. Age in years: _____

2. Age I feel: _____

3. Grade/level: _____

4. School I attend (circle one if in school):
   • public
   • private
   • homeschool
   • college
   • write in school name: _____

5. Eye color: _____

6. Hair color: _____

7. Skin color: _____

8. I live with: _____

9. City, state, country I live in: _____

10. Geographic region is called: _____

11. Family of origin is from: _____

12. Immigration status: _____

13. Race/ethnicity/culture/tribal affiliation: _____

14. Religion/spirituality: _____

15. People in my family (given or chosen): _____

    _____

16. Number of siblings: _____

17. Social class of my family of origin: _____

18. I live in a(n): apartment, house, condo, mobile home, other type of home, currently experiencing or have experienced homelessness.

19. Romantic orientation (separate from sexual orientation): no romantic attraction, some romantic attraction, Where are my roses?!?

20. Gender identity (separate from sexual orientation): Do you have feelings about identifying your gender? Why do you think that is? Remember, if it doesn't feel safe or you prefer not to identify, skip it! See the glossary for definitions.
    - agender
    - androgyne or androgynous
    - bigender
    - cisgender
    - gender expansive
    - gender fluid
    - genderqueer
    - non-binary
    - pangender
    - questioning
    - transgender/trans (write in more specific identities below)
    - Two Spirit
    - prefer not to label myself
    - write in: _____

21. Gender expression (behavior, clothing/style, haircut, voice; may or may not be in alignment with gender identity):
    - femme
    - feminine
    - masculine
    - butch
    - creative expression
    - androgynous
    - gender nonconforming
    - fluid
    - gender expansive
    - genderqueer
    - gender fabulous!
    - prefer not to label myself
    - write in: _____

22. Sexual orientation (separate from gender identity): Do you have feelings about identifying your sexuality? Again, if it doesn't feel safe or you prefer not to identify, skip it!
    - lesbian
    - gay
    - bisexual
    - queer
    - questioning
    - asexual
    - pansexual
    - demisexual
    - straight
    - prefer not to label myself
    - write in: _____

23. Body size/type/feelings about body: Can you appreciate and/ or accept your body (even if you may want to change it)? What are things you like about your body _____ _____

24. Speaking up: prefer behind the scenes, grab the mic!

25. Personality type: dominant, aggressive, assertive, laid back, nurturer "mother hen," group guide

26. Dominant hand: left, right, ambidextrous

27. Hobbies: _____

28. Relationship preference: single, dating, coupled, polyamorous or non-monogamous (multiple partners/relationships), monogamous (one partner/relationship)

29. Athletic: prefer to play, prefer to watch (which sports?): _____ _____ , not my thing

30. Creative/artistic? Which field/medium? _____ _____ , not my thing

31. Verbal/linguistic: I speak/sign which language(s): _____ _____

32. Ability/disability: _____

33. Visual/spatial: _____

34. Auditory/musical: _____

35. Prefer hands-on? Let's make something! I don't want to get my hands dirty.

36. Social learning: group projects, study buddies, flying solo

37. Movement preference: dance, gym, sporty, I'd rather sit this one out, thanks

38. Health status/issues: _____

39. Mental health status/issues: _____

40. Family health or mental health issues: _____
_____

41. Introvert (gets energy from being alone), extrovert (gets energy from being with others), ambivert (a blend)

42. Interpersonal skill level: I can't get enough of people, "People scare me!", neutral

43. Intrapersonal skill level: Mindfulness is my jam! I reflect on myself. I'd rather not pay attention to myself. I am my own friend. I love myself. I am learning to love myself.

44. Parent(s)/guardian(s) marital status: married, divorced, unmarried, single, not applicable, not known

45. Parent(s)/guardian(s)/grandparents are: strict, traditional, open-minded, accepting, mixed responses

46. Pet(s)/animal companions: I'm allergic. I have a fur-baby. My house has more animals than people. I do not have animals.

47. Neurodiversity: autistic, allistic (non-autistic), ADHD, dyslexic, write in: _____

48. Learning difference(s): _____
_____

49. Assistive devices/technology: glasses, hearing aids/cochlear implants, cane, wheelchair, crutches, walker, speech board, write in: _____

50. Public speaking: Love it! Please don't make me! If necessary...

51. Tech savvy: Tech master! I click what?!?

52. Ever moved? frequently, never, once, twice, a few times

53. Extended family: We're close. I don't have any idea if I have extended family.

54. Travel: I've barely left my block, frequent flyer (name places you've been) _____

    _____

55. Friends: one, many, none, a few close friends, I want some friends, I prefer to be by myself

56. Career interest: _____

57. Favorite type/genre of music: _____

58. Favorite food: _____

59. Like to cook? Top chef! Where do I find a spoon?

60. Tidy/messy room: _____

61. Ever broken a bone? _____

62. Sense of humor: love to laugh, this is serious! jokester/class clown, punster

63. Fashion/style: _____

64. How I feel about school:
    • I love learning.
    • I'm in it for the social time.
    • School is not my thing.
    • I can learn anything.

- Why bother when there's the internet and calculators?
- I can't wait to graduate!
- Write in: _____

65. Experienced trauma (accident, violence, etc.)? _____
    _____

66. Favorite color: _____

67. Orientation to change: I like things as they are. Bring it on! I'm flexible.

68. Involved in politics:
    - concerned about social justice
    - care about equal rights
    - concerned about the environment
    - concerned about the economy
    - interested in news
    - activist
    - uninterested
    - write in: _____

69. Miscellaneous: perfectionist, procrastinator, organized, messy, sensitive, intuitive, cynical, sarcastic

70. Receiving feedback: open to ideas, have a hard time with criticism, neutral

71. What else is important to you? Write in: _____
    _____

72. What is missing from this list? Write in: _____
    _____

Wow! That was some list! There are more than 70 categories for each person. Of those categories, what do we know about a person just from looking? What do we assume about a person? Why do we make those assumptions? Are we interested in learning more about people or are we attached to the boxes to which we have limited them? Are we attached to the boxes into which we put ourselves? Are we open to change? Do we struggle with or accept change in others? Do we struggle with or accept change within ourselves?

The possibilities are endless!

If each of the 70+ identity categories had five possibilities (even though some identity categories may have more and some may have fewer options) and we wanted to determine the total number of possibilities, we would multiply 5 by itself 70 times. That would be over a quindecillion (a number with 48 zeros)! How can we even begin to wrap our brains around a number that represents the possible human identity diversity? We are considering a number that is greater than the number of people on Earth (7.7 billion), greater than the billions of stars in our solar system, greater than the trillions of cells in the human body, and greater than the quintillions of grains of sand on Earth. We don't even have a comparison for how big 70 categories of five possibilities each represents! Let's just say it is astronomical! If you love math and science, look online to see if you can find something in the natural world with that many possibilities. With all of our various identities and personal traits, we can definitely say that each person is a unique universe! Wow!

DRAW YOURSELF!

Sketch a picture of yourself and some of your personal identities and traits. Add some details to the picture that represent things that are important to you like people, places, animals, food, and hobbies. Maybe you love drawing. Maybe not. Do you want to skip this activity because it scares you? That's certainly an option. Try it anyway! Have fun with it. Use color if you want. Relax and create!

Diversity abounds! There is beauty in the diversity of nature and in humans. The differences are what make us interesting! If you assume anything about people, assume that there are numerous ways a person could be at this moment and that they may change in the future. It could take a lifetime just to get to know yourself, so enjoy the process! All people and all genders are wanted, needed, and valued.

Let's play a guessing game!

GUESS WHICH GENDER ADVERTISING WOULD BE DIRECTED TOWARDS

1. Dolls

2. Basketball sneakers

3. Dresses

4. Baseball hats

5. Hooded sweatshirts

6. Fuzzy slippers

7. Nail polish

8. Toy cars or trucks

9. Makeup

10. Toy robots

11. Science kits

12. Beads

13. Magic tricks

> **Please note that the answers will follow immediately afterwards. Hey, no peeking!**

1. Dolls: Girls
2. Basketball sneakers: Boys
3. Dresses: Girls
4. Baseball hats: Boys
5. Hooded sweat-shirts: Boys
6. Fuzzy slippers: Girls
7. Nail polish: Girls
8. Toy cars or trucks: Boys
9. Makeup: Girls
10. Toy robots: Boys
11. Science kits: Boys
12. Beads: Girls
13. Magic tricks: Boys

Note: the *actual* market for each of these items is *everyone of all genders*!

Why is there a gender associated with these items? Who benefits from this division of toys, clothes, and accessories? Does any human really need polished nails? If we say that it is for the sake of beauty or artistry, then wouldn't nail polish look good on any finger or toe regardless of gender? Why does this idea make some people so uncomfortable?

Most people in the United States have been taught from birth that there are two genders: male and female. This is referred to as the gender binary. Further, we are taught that these genders have expectations for behavior, dress, and body. Are we taught these things in school? Not explicitly/directly. There is not usually a lesson on gender expectations like there are reading or math lessons. We get these messages from the images we see and the way society is set up (for example, toy or clothing stores, language, bathrooms, and the ways that people respond to each other). Gender markers (such as a check box for male or female) are everywhere: birth certificates, driver's licenses, school records and identification cards, medical records, job applications, college applications, passports, and so on!

GENDER BINARY IMPACT CHECKLIST

How do you experience the gender binary? Check the options which apply right now (subject to future change).

- ☐ I am not personally impacted by the gender binary.
- ☐ I am personally impacted by the social enforcement of the gender binary.
- ☐ I don't know anyone who is impacted by the gender binary.
- ☐ I care about people who are negatively impacted by the social enforcement of the gender binary.

What is your perspective on the gender binary? Check the options which apply right now (subject to future change).

- ☐ I need a definition. I am not even sure I understand what those words mean. See glossary.
- ☐ I see a system of two genders as neutral or beneficial.
- ☐ I am beginning to understand the impacts of the social enforcement of the gender binary.
- ☐ I am a change-maker around gender. I take action to make sure people of all genders are included, safe, and welcome in my family, school, community, and world.
- ☐ Write in: _____
  _____
  _____
  _____

Whether we recognize it or not, the gender binary operates in all of our lives. It is a system of privilege, power, advantage, and harm.

Gender is a social construct. What does that mean? A set of people (usually "experts") decides that certain aspects or features are classified as a particular group. Businesses market their services and products to this group. Institutions of society (such as schools, laws, jobs, housing, family, and religion) are formed around this grouping. Many people who feel comfortable with the grouping go along with this idea without questioning whether the model fits everyone well and whether it is helpful or harmful to have this designation. Even though something is constructed, it can still have significant consequences in society. Some people who are harmed by the grouping work towards bringing awareness to the injustice and changing the model. A social construct creates an arbitrary division among people. People's attachment to the construct and discomfort with anything outside of those strictly defined categories is what can cause harm.

It is important to remember that humans created the current gender binary and we have the power to change that system. Social change takes time and effort. We hope that you have the patience and determination to commit to being a Super Trans Ally for the long term.

What is the difference between gender identity and gender expression?

Gender identity refers to how a person feels and thinks about themself. Gender expression includes clothing, demeanor, style, voice tone, and even how we move our bodies and take up space in the world. We get to see the way that someone expresses their gender by outward signs but we may not know how that person identifies within themself. We cannot make assumptions. We'll talk more about assumptions in Chapter 5.

WHY ARE SOME PEOPLE UPSET BY GENDER DIVERSITY?

When someone believes strongly in the gender binary, they may have a reaction when that system is questioned. Sometimes those responses can include fear, hate, and violence. This is called transphobia. Why are people so invested in the strict enforcement of the gender binary?

What is your experience? Check the options that apply right now (subject to future change).

☐ I have experienced a negative reaction within myself when someone's gender expression was different from what I assumed about their gender.
☐ My friends or family have a hard time understanding transgender, gender expansive, or non-binary gender expressions/presentations.

☐ I am concerned for my friend(s) and/or family member(s) who are transgender, non-binary, or gender expansive. I don't want them to experience bullying/harassment or violence.

☐ I really don't understand why people are so invested in a system that causes harm.

☐ I take actions towards creating a home, school, and world which are inclusive of all genders.

We are each comprised of our many identities. At times, we may feel that one identity is primary. We really cannot define people or make assumptions about them just because we know one or more of their identities. We certainly cannot separate out one or some of a person's identity categories because all of our identities combined are part of our whole experience.

THE GENDER UNIVERSE

What comes to mind when you hear the words "infinite possibilities"? Observe any thoughts or feelings you may have. Does it cause an overwhelming sensation? Does it spark excitement? Notice any visuals that initially popped into your mind. Do you see yourself in a spaceship exploring the unknown? Did an image of an unlimited lunch buffet come to mind? Did you see yourself stretching your arms and hands out high towards the sky to symbolize endless possibilities in your life? What sounds did you hear, if any, when you pictured those two words? Say them out loud if you want. Infinite possibilities. Say them again if you'd like. Infinite possibilities... Perhaps it goes beyond what we can even imagine could be reality. How do you experience the words "gender universe"? What does it mean to you? *Gender universe encompasses a world with infinite possibilities for how we may identify, experience, and express our gender!* It's a beautiful, colorful gender universe with rainbow sprinkles of people with diverse upbringings, experiences, ideas, values, beliefs, expressions, and so much more.

Look around you and outside of you. Listen to what is near to you and beyond you. Be open to thinking differently about things. Nothing is written with permanent ink. Preconceived notions can transform into new perceptions when we are open to infinite possibilities. The way we feel on the inside and how we want to express ourselves on the outside can change. We do not have to be who others tell us we are or are supposed to be. We do not have to think the way others tells us or expect us to think. We each have our own mind and heart and the right to think and feel the way we naturally do, and the way we choose to. At different times in our life we may feel as if we are being forced to have to choose or not choose and it may not feel right to us or organic. Our mind and heart are meant to grow and expand throughout our life. We may have been taught that there are only two genders that a person can be given when they are born and that it stays that way for the rest of our lives. We may also have been taught that there are very specific expectations, roles, and forms of expression that are acceptable for these two genders. The gender universe teaches us that there are many genders that people identify as and with, and there are astronomical ways in which a person may express their gender or just express themself regardless of gender. You may have always known this depending on what you have been taught and experienced or you may have discovered this at some point in your life. For some of you, that time is now. Everyone deserves to feel free to be their authentic self. Whether you feel like the gender you were given at birth or a different gender among the hundreds of other genders that are equally valid in our gender universe, we see you. You are shining bright and highly visible, valuable, and lovable just the way you are!

MY GENDER EXPERIENCES CHECKLIST

How do you identify your gender?

- ☐ I have never questioned my gender identity. The gender that was assigned to me at birth feels right to me (cisgender/cis).
- ☐ I have questioned my gender and currently identify as cis.
- ☐ I am currently questioning my gender identity.
- ☐ I identify as genderqueer, gender fluid, gender expansive, transgender, non-binary, gender fabulous, or another gender.
- ☐ I identify as agender (without gender).
- ☐ I do not participate in the gender binary.
- ☐ I prefer not to identify. Don't box me in!
- ☐ It's not safe for me to share this.
- ☐ Write in: _____

_____

How often do you think about how you express your gender?

- ☐ I have never thought about this before.
- ☐ I think about my gender expression all the time.
- ☐ When there is a special occasion, I think about how I will dress or expectations for how I will behave.
- ☐ Write in: _____

_____

JOURNAL PROMPT: HOW DO YOU LIKE TO EXPRESS YOUR GENDER?

If there were no social expectations for how you dress, talk, move, act, create, or consume (food, music, movies, books, interests, toys), what would you do? Would you make the same choices you make now? How would you behave? How would you look? How would you feel? Write your responses below or write in your personal journal or type your responses or record a voice memo.

_____

_____

_____

YES, NO, OR MAYBE SO? WHAT DO YOU THINK ABOUT GENDER?

Respond to each statement with a tick in the "Yes," "No," or "Maybe so" column.

	Yes	No	Maybe so
1. Gender identity and gender expression are always aligned. If a person feels like a certain gender, they also show outward signs of that gender.			
2. Everyone has a right to define their own gender.			
3. Gender and sexuality are linked. Anyone who identifies as transgender likes to date the "opposite" sex.			
4. Anyone who identifies as agender (without gender) also identifies as asexual (without sexual attraction).			
5. Gender is a fixed identity for life.			
6. People who identify as gender nonconforming also identify as transgender.			
7. Trans girls or trans women always wear makeup.			
8. Everyone should conform to society's gender binary expectations.			
9. Intersex people (born with various combinations of genitals, sex chromosomes, and hormones) can decide as they grow up how they identify their gender.			
10. Effeminate men are always gay and butch women are always lesbians.			

> **Please note that the answers will follow immediately afterwards. Hey, no peeking!**

Let's discuss each of the items in the "Yes, No, or Maybe so."

1. No, because of the word "always." There are times, places, and people with whom we may not feel comfortable expressing our gender identity.

2. "Everyone has a right to define their own gender." Yes!

3. No. How we express ourselves and who we love are not linked. We are unique universes!

4. No, because this is a blanket generalization. Some agender people may identify as asexual.

5. Maybe so. For some people this is true. For some people this is not at all true.

6. Maybe so. This is true for some people but not for others. Some butch women may identify as gender nonconforming but not as trans. They still identify as women.

7. No. Makeup is or should be a choice and not socially enforced based on gender.

8. No. This is the source of harm for many people.

9. Maybe so. Many intersex people have been assumed a binary sex (male or female) at birth and received medical interventions without their consent. Some intersex people have the opportunity to express their gender in an organic way.

10. No. Can we avoid assumptions based on gender stereotypes? Gender and sexual orientation are separate.

Each person is a unique universe. *You* are a unique universe. How does it feel to be you? Only you can answer that. Get to know yourself more and more. Find ways to appreciate and love yourself.

LET'S DANCE!

. . . .

Let's dance to feel our bodies and hearts! Put on your favorite music and move in ways that feel good to you. Be in the moment and the movement and just have fun. If you like to dance on your own, do that. If you like to have others with you, invite them. If you can move in ways that you have never moved before, you'll learn something new about yourself. Explore. Release judgment and fear. Sing out loud while you dance if you dare. Breathe deeply. Be yourself.

We are lucky to live in a world with so much diversity! Each of us is a unique universe and we are all on this planet together at this time. Can we find ways to accept, appreciate, and celebrate ourselves and each other? Yes, please! Can we make the world a safer and more welcoming place? Yes, we can! Let's work together as Super Trans Allies to be in our fullest creative expression and lead with love.

CHAPTER 3

Your Loved One Is Trans and They Still Love the Same Colors!

When a friend, sibling, or loved one comes out as being trans, it's natural to have an influx of thoughts and questions running through your head!

★ What does this mean for my friend, sibling, or loved one? What does this mean for me and for the relationship?

★ Does my trans loved one want to be called a different name?

★ Does my genderqueer sibling want to use different pronouns?

★ Does my gender fluid cousin want to wear different clothing?

★ Does my gender expansive friend like different colors? Different activities and hobbies? Different foods? Different music and movie genres? Different characters in video games?

★ Does my non-binary parent have different types of people they are attracted to?

The answer to all of your questions is...**we don't know**...until the person tells you! For some people, when they begin to explore their gender and/or arrive at a gender destination that feels just right to them, they might change the way they view or experience things they once liked or disliked. For others, they may still like or dislike the same things as they did before they came to this realization about their gender or before their gender exploration journey began.

Rather than make any assumptions, you can just ask them! It's a great way to show support for an important trans person in your life, and to go beyond by showing them that you are genuinely interested in learning more about their experience. So, take out your smartphone, iPad, laptop, or paper and pen if you're old school! Let's practice. You've got this!

BUBBLE GUM: CONNECT
• •

Find time to get together in person and learn more about the experience and needs of the trans and gender diverse people in your life! Come up with your own approach for asking your questions. You may choose to keep it simple and to the point with a list of questions that you cross off as you go. Keep in mind that open-ended questions (not a yes/no question) could provide you with more details. You may choose to have your questions on a large piece of chart paper and to ask your trans friend to write the answers next to each question with scented colored markers. You could even choose to sing your questions and ask your trans loved one to answer them using interpretive dance! You know this person best, so go with what feels right to you. Be sure to ask them if the approach works for them, too!

Other things to consider are when and where you will have this conversation. Come up with a space and time that works for both of you. Do you want to chat in private or while sipping on tea or hot chocolate in a cafe? Will the whipped cream on your nose be a distraction from a more serious conversation? Perhaps, or maybe it will make you both laugh and feel less nervous. There is no wrong or right way to do this as long as you both agree on something! Here are some sample non-assumptive questions using different styles of approaching the topic of a favorite color:

★ Is your favorite color still red? If not, what is it now?
★ If you were a crayon, what color would you be and why?
★ If you could paint the town any color, what would it be?
★ Your birthday is coming up and I know you need a new shirt! What color shirt do you want?
★ Have you experienced any changes in the colors you like? If so, what's changed?
★ Start singing Cyndi Lauper's timeless song "True Colors." Then ask, what are your true favorite colors?

Here is another example of questions surrounding the topic of activities and hobbies:

★ Friday is BFFMN (Best Friends Forever Movie Night). Do you want to see a romantic drama or a horror flick? Or both or a different genre?
★ We've been playing on the boys' baseball team since we were both nine years old. Are you going to continue to play on the boys' team, the girls' team, neither, both, or something else?
★ What activities do you like now? The same ones or different ones? Tell me about what you like.
★ If I could get tickets to any sporting event, what sport would you choose?
★ When we play video games, which character will you choose? Will you play one that is gendered or non-gendered or mixed or something else?

Now it's your turn to practice! Your topic is **clothing**. Take your time and list a few of your questions below:

1. _____

2. _____

3. _____

4. _____

You can do this for any topic. You can get as creative as you wish, as long as your friend says it's OK to ask them questions in the format you choose. If you are an artist who draws portraits and needs models for art class or for a school fashion show fundraiser, you may also decide to ask your friend to be your model. Ask them to rock out in whatever fashion and style that feels most comfortable for them!

ERASE-A-SKETCH-A-SSUMPTIONS AWAY!

Here is an exercise that may help you to clear your mind of any preconceived notions about gender, gender expression, transitioning, and overall trans experience.

Imagine your mind as a mind/mental Erase-a-Sketch, similar to that red, rectangular, timeless toy, the Etch-a-Sketch™. You may recall that you can turn the knobs to create words and images that will stay on the screen until you shake the toy and erase what you wrote or drew. It's a pretty cool toy and one that is for everyone of every age! Now, imagine that your mind is an Erase-a-Sketch. For this exercise, try to imagine that your mind is full of thoughts, words, and images related to gender expression, gender identity, trans experience, gender binary vs. non-binary, and transitioning from one gender to another. You have been accumulating these thoughts and beliefs since you were born, based on your personal experiences, what you've been told, what you have learned, and what has been etched in your mind over time. We bet your screen is so full that there is not much space left! It's possible that it may be hard to see the difference between what you were taught to believe, what you have learned on your own, what you believe to be true, what you are still exploring, and what are questions you still have that are unanswered.

After each word or phrase below, fill your mind Erase-a-Sketch with any words, feelings, and/or images that come to your brain. Try not to think too hard about it and allow the words/images to flow naturally.

Words/phrases:

- Change from one gender to a different one
- Trans and transitioning
- Trans boy interests and activities

- Trans girl hair and clothing
- Non-binary and public restrooms
- Gender fluid expression
- Queer and trans and dating

Now, shake it all out until you erase those thoughts and feelings. Erase-a-Sketch-a-ssumptions away! Now that you have a blank screen again, try to put yourself in the shoes of someone who is trans. Imagine what they may be thinking about and experiencing. Do their thoughts, feelings, actions, and interests change when their gender changes? Making assumptions about people based on one component of their identity can be limiting and potentially make a trans person feel as if they need to fit into a one-size-fits-all box to be affirmed for who they are. Do all boys who were assumed to be male at birth have short hair and wear football jerseys? Do all girls who were assumed to be female at birth like pink, shopping, and makeup? Not at all!

The same is true for someone who identifies as trans or a different gender from the one they were thought to be at birth. A person who is trans and male does not always want to cut their hair short, wear baggy clothes, play sports, or have a deeper voice. A person who is trans and female does not always want to wear lipstick and dresses, have longer hair, and have no facial or body hair. Someone who is non-binary and identifies as neither male nor female or both doesn't have to look androgynous or a certain way to be non-binary. Ultimately, there is no Erase-a-Sketch that can reflect the diverse experiences of all trans people. Your Erase-a-Sketches come from your own feelings, thoughts, interpretations, assumptions, perceptions, and experience. Now it's time to create new Erase-a-Sketches based on the actual experiences of a trans person. If you have an important trans person in your life, ask them if you can do an activity with them that will help you to understand more about their unique experience of being trans.

Are you ready to Erase-a-Sketch-a-ssumptions away?

If possible, you can have paper with boxes drawn to symbolize the mind Erase-a-Sketch. Let your trans friend or family member know that you will say words and phrases and ask that they respond with words and/or descriptions and visualizations of how those words pertain to their experience as a trans person. For each phrase, fill in one of the boxes with the words and visual representations that your trans loved one uses to describe their experience.

Here is the list of words/phrases again:

- Change from one gender to a different one
- Trans and transitioning
- Trans boy interests and activities
- Trans girl hair and clothing
- Non-binary and public restrooms
- Gender fluid expression
- Queer and trans and dating

You can try this with one person or try it with all of the trans and gender-fabulous people in your life!

Some questions to ask yourself afterwards:

1. Did your friend's responses surprise you or challenge your assumptions?

2. Did their unique experiences help you to understand the range of trans experience?

3. Did this activity change your way of thinking about the list of words/phrases?

BUBBLE GUM: AFFIRM

. . . .

After your friend, sibling, relative, or loved one comes out as trans, here are some general ideas for things you can say and do that may be fun and really affirming:

1. How about we go clothes shopping this weekend? We can check out whatever stores and styles of clothing you want, and I'll stand by the waiting room if you want to show them off and get my input! It'll be your own fashion show!

2. I know that we have been going to baseball practice every day after school together for the past month, but I want you to know that I support any decision you make either to stay on the baseball team or to switch over to the softball team, or to do both or neither. I've got your back!

3. I know that purple has been your favorite color since you were two years old. Mom said she was getting you a scarf and gloves for the holidays. Are you still cool with purple or should I nudge her to get a different color?

4. If you ever need me to get you anything that may be uncomfortable for you, like certain monthly products or other more personal and private things, let me know, OK?

5. You're such a talented singer and have an awesome range. If you would rather be something else instead of soprano in choir, I'd totally go with you to talk to the choir director.

6. For prom, all the girls in our group are going to get a manicure the day before. I don't want to assume that you don't want to go. I think nail polish looks good on anyone of any gender. They have all colors, even black and clear, or sparkles if you want!

7. We can still do our weekend sleepovers. My parents might make us sleep in separate rooms, but we can still watch movies, eat junk food, and play our favorite video games.

8. I want you to know that you can talk to me about anything, including the people you are attracted to. I support you if you are into cisgender people, non-binary people, trans people, or all of the above. We can always talk about stuff like that and it will never be weird. I am your best friend and I can still tell you who I think will be good enough for you!

One of the most important things you can do for trans people in your life is to not make assumptions about personal needs, desires, and interests, whether it be before, during, or after transition from one gender to a different one or without transitioning at all. Not everyone likes clothing, activities, roles, or colors that are stereotypically associated with a particular gender. Do you ever wonder if babies could talk, what would they say about the bombardment of blue and pink everything in their new world? Perhaps they would prefer yellow or orange or different colors? Maybe they wouldn't even care because they would rather be bombarded with food, kisses, and love. And maybe they would rather be burped than bombarded by anything at all!

CHAPTER 4

When We Say Everybody Is Included, We Mean Every BODY!

One of the many beautiful things about being you is that *you* truly are special! Your unique blueprint is a combination of different components that may reflect who you are and how you identify now or at any given point. Depending on your experience and beliefs, these components may include your mind, body, spirit, genetics, personality, expression, or any of the multiple layers of identity such as race, ethnicity, gender assigned at birth, gender identity, gender expression, sexual orientation, ability/disability, mental health, country of origin, immigration status, language, socioeconomic status, and many more layers of you.

Some parts of who you are now may be things that have been with you from the time you were born and will stay part of you for your entire life. Many pieces of your identity are not fixed. These are things that can and may change at some point in your life. You are always evolving and your experience as it relates to your mind, body, spirit, and any of the other layers of your identity may change at any point in your life! Your feelings, thoughts, and experience surrounding who you are and how you self-identify may change once, twice, or even multiple times. These changes may be permanent or they may be fluid. There is no wrong way to experience change. No other person can tell you how to think, feel, experience, identify, or express yourself. Only you can determine what feels right and comfortable, and feels like the best fit for you!

IDENTITY: FIXED OR FLUID?

Which parts of your identity do you think won't change in your lifetime?

-------------------------   -------------------------

-------------------------   -------------------------

Which parts of your identity do you think could be fluid or change at some point in your life?

-------------------------   -------------------------

-------------------------   -------------------------

When it comes to certain parts of your identity, some people will question you. They may question how you know who you are and why you feel or think a certain way, dress or look a certain way, like or dislike certain things, and make the decisions you make.

Has anyone ever said to you, "You are too young to know who you are!"?

What are the first words and/or feelings that came to mind when you read or hear this statement?

You may have had a response in mind such as "It's none of your business! I know who I am!" That is a completely normal and human response. It can feel like a personal attack when someone doubts that you can know who you are just because you are younger.

Think of someone important in your life whom you consider family, given or chosen. Imagine that you are having a conversation and they ask you a number of questions about you and your experiences and/or choices. For each question and statement below, fill in the blank with how you would feel, what you would think, and/or what you might say in response to the questions.

1. Why do you dress like that? What kind of look is that?

----

2. Why do you color your hair blue? What's wrong with your natural color?

----

3. Why do you wear so much makeup and cover up your nice face?

Those were examples of questions that parent(s) and other adult family members may ask you and other young people.

JUDGMENTAL QUESTIONS

Now, imagine (if you do not self-identify this way already) that you are also transgender, non-binary, or any of the other gender-fabulous identities. Here are some of the questions gender diverse people may get asked.

1. Why do you wear eyeliner and lipstick if you are a boy now?

2. How am I supposed to think of you or look at you as a girl if you don't dress like one?

3. How am I supposed to remember to call you he or him when you still have a girl voice?

4. How can you pass as a boy with your chest?

5. Why don't you cut your hair short if you are a boy and want people to see you that way?

The reality is that these are frequent questions that trans and non-binary people experience on a regular basis. You may or may not have had these thoughts or questions for the trans, non-binary, and gender expansive people in your life or in general, but many others do.

It's natural to have questions. Before asking them, think about how it may potentially be perceived by the person. Could it be hurtful? Could it come across as judgmental?

COLORING INSIDE OF THE LINES

Most people in our society believe that gender exists as a binary and that people are either female/girl/woman or male/boy/man. Even for those who believe that transgender identities exist, they still may subscribe to this binary system of gender. As you may recall, this is a system that reflects only two genders with many restrictions and expectations for both females/girls/women and for males/boys/men. Match the physical characteristics, personality traits, and forms of expression below with male/boy/man or female/girl/woman based on expectations that our current society has about boys/men and girls/women. List any or all under either male/boy/man or female/girl/woman based on what cultural expectations exist. This may or may not reflect what you believe to be true about people who identify as male/boy/man or female/girl/woman.

Physical characteristics	Personality traits	Forms of expression
Facial hair	Sensitive	Plays football
Body hair	Strong	Wears pink
Tall	Nurturing	Dance/ballet
Short hair	Funny	Wears nail polish
Long hair	Brave	Plays video games
Soft skin	Leader	Theater
Muscles	Confident	Likes princesses
Flat chest	Intelligent	Baking
Deep voice	Creative	Likes romantic
Higher-pitched voice	Charming	comedies
Large hands	Inspiring	Has ears pierced
Athletic body	Talented	Choir
Toned body	Patient	Plays with dolls
High cheekbones	Caring	Likes glitter
Belly fat	Empathetic	Boxing
	Weak	Sits with legs crossed
	Insecure	Wears makeup
	Artistic	Likes action movies
		Likes shopping

Now, list all of the characteristics, traits, and forms of expression that are expectations of what is appropriate and acceptable for females/girls/women and for males/boys/men by society's standards in the context of a binary system:

WHEN WE SAY EVERYBODY IS INCLUDED, WE MEAN EVERY BODY!

female/girl/woman   **male/boy/man**

_____   _____

_____   _____

_____   _____

_____   _____

_____   _____

_____   _____

_____   _____

_____   _____

_____   _____

_____   _____

_____   _____

_____   _____

_____   _____

Questions:

1. What assumptions do people make about girls/women and boys/men?

2. Do you think that a person's gender expression is related to their gender identity, and if so, in what ways?

While there is a lot of work still to be done, many more people are understanding and accepting gender as a spectrum beyond the binary and into outer space with hundreds of gender identities that exist. For the gender identities below, list the physical characteristics, personality traits, and forms of expression that could fall under each. Base this on your own beliefs about gender.

Cisgender boy/man

Physical characteristics:

Personality traits:

Gender/creative expression:

_____

_____

_____

Cisgender girl/woman

Physical characteristics:

_____

_____

_____

Personality traits:

_____

_____

_____

Gender/creative expression:

_____

_____

_____

Transgender male and/or boy and/or man

Physical characteristics:

_____

_____

_____

Personality traits:

_____

_____

_____

Gender/creative expression:

_____

_____

_____

Transgender female and/or girl and/or woman

Physical characteristics:

_____

_____

_____

Personality traits:

_____

_____

_____

Gender/creative expression:

_____

_____

_____

Non-binary person

Physical characteristics:

_____

_____

_____

Personality traits:

_____

_____

_____

Gender/creative expression:

We all have preconceived notions about gender and perhaps even about how people should look, act, talk, walk, and be in this world based on their gender. Some of those preconceived notions that we have are shifting and, in some cases, fading away. There are many factors that influence these changes. Regardless of why and how, what is most important as an ally is to accept a whole person without letting those preconceived notions get in the way. Preconceived notions, stereotypes, assumptions, and expectations are things that limit people and can also contribute to harming people. Just as there is a lot of diversity among people in general, there is also a lot of diversity among subcommunities, including within transgender and non-binary communities. Not every trans person has the same experience!

PORTRAITS OF DIVERSE TRANS AND NON-BINARY EXPERIENCES

To help us to become more mindful that trans and non-binary people experience their gender in unique ways, here are a few generalized examples of gender diverse people with a description of their experiences. Below each example, please identify some actions that may have been taken or that can potentially be taken by parent(s)/guardian(s), family, school, employers, and community members to best support each person around their transition and/or experience.

Transgender identities

1. Morgan is a 23-year-old Black transgender gay male. He was thought to be female when he was born. Morgan uses he/him pronouns. After college he started his gender transition. For him this meant coming out as trans to family, friends, and community as well as changing his name and pronouns. He started the hormone testosterone a year ago. He had a desire to experience changes in his voice and hoped to have more face and body hair. He has also had top surgery. At this time, he feels that he has completed his transition and identifies as a man. He had been out as being gay at the school he teaches at and just came out last week as also being trans.

   a. Supportive actions taken by school:

   ----

   b. Supportive actions taken by community:

   ----

2. Allison is a 12-year-old white trans girl. She was thought to be male when she was born, but at the age of five, she started to tell her mom, who is a single parent, and everyone at school that she was a girl. With the support of her mom and

a trans-affirming therapist, Allison started a hormone blocker that would prevent her from going into the incorrect puberty and allow her to enter into the correct one that affirms her gender. Her mom also consented to changing her name and gender marker legally.

a. Supportive actions taken by school:

----

b. Supportive actions taken by friends:

----

3. Yuan is a 17-year-old Chinese American trans boy. Yuan was thought to be female when he was born. Yuan prefers to be referred to just by name and does not use any set of pronouns. Yuan has never had the desire to start hormone treatment or undergo any medical surgery. Yuan kept the name Yuan since the name felt gender-neutral. Yuan is part of a comedy troupe and recently let the group know to just use Yuan's name and no pronouns from now on.

a. Supportive actions taken by parent(s)/guardian(s):

----

b. Supportive actions taken by school:

Non-binary identities

1. Em is 14 years old, Latinx, and non-binary. Em's pronouns are they/them. They just came out this year as feeling like they are neither a boy nor a girl. Em has asked their friends to use they/them and has come out as non-binary to their dad. He has been supportive, but Em's mom is less supportive and continues to use she/her to refer to Em. It's been challenging at family events because of the mixed support from their parents.

   a. Supportive actions taken by friends:

   _____

   _____

   b. Supportive actions taken by school:

   _____

   _____

2. Zan is 19 years old, Jewish, and self-identifies as genderqueer. Zan uses both sets of pronouns he/him and she/her depending on how Zan is feeling at the time. Zan is taking the hormone testosterone. She has not had surgery but is considering top surgery in the future. He works in customer service at a local coffee shop and finds it challenging explaining gender fluidity to his co-workers. Zan is also not her legal name at this time due to financial barriers to getting it changed.

   a. Supportive actions taken by employer/co-workers:

   _____

   _____

  b. Supportive actions taken by community:

  ----

3. Ozzie is 29 years old, Cherokee, uses the pronouns zie/hir, and self-identifies as Two Spirit. Zie is a nurse at a local children's hospital. Ozzie believes that zie embraces both hir femininity and masculinity at the same time. Zie gets asked by young patients daily if zie is a boy or a girl. Ozzie has to follow a strict gendered dress code at work.

  a. Supportive actions taken by employer/co-workers:

  ----

  b. Supportive actions taken by community:

If you ask 100 trans people how they would describe being trans, you could get 100 different ways people would describe their trans experience. You would also see that trans and non-binary people have different needs and desires pertaining to how they feel on the inside as it relates or doesn't relate to how they want to be perceived and express themselves on the outside to the rest of the world. For some people, the way they express themselves is connected to their to gender identity. For others, the way they express themselves is not tied to their gender identity. It may just be the way a person feels comfortable and likes to express themself. Some trans and non-binary people have the desire to make legal changes such as a change in name or gender marker, make physical changes such as top surgery or taking hormones, and make other changes like pronouns, the clothes they wear, the style of their hair, or the way they speak. Some trans and non-binary people have no desire to make any legal, medical, or social changes now or possibly ever in their lifetime. The gender of any person is not defined by a name, pronouns, body, genitalia, hormones, voice, hobby, or anything else. It is who we know we are on the inside, and how we express our gender or express ourselves varies across and within all genders.

Keeping this in mind, let's go back to the previous activity and try the last part again, but this time select physical characteristics, personality traits, and forms of expression from more than one gender and combine them for each of the genders. For example, if you start with "cisgender male/boy/man," you would select physical characteristics listed under "cisgender male/boy/man," "cisgender female/girl/woman," "transgender male/boy/man," "transgender female/girl/woman," and "non-binary person." You would do the same for personality traits and for forms of expression. Follow the same instructions for the rest of the genders. When you are finished listing them out, you can opt to reflect the new characteristics, traits, and expression for each gender in a picture.

RE-DO! COLORING OUTSIDE OF THE LINES
• •

Cisgender boy/man

Physical characteristics:

_____

_____

_____

Personality traits:

_____

_____

_____

Gender/creative expression:

_____

_____

_____

Cisgender girl/woman

Physical characteristics:

Personality traits:

Gender/creative expression:

Transgender male and/or boy and/or man

Physical characteristics:

Personality traits:

Gender/creative expression:

Transgender female and/or girl and/or woman

Physical characteristics:

_____

_____

_____

Personality traits:

_____

_____

_____

Gender/creative expression:

_____

_____

_____

Non-binary person

Physical characteristics:

Personality traits:

Gender/creative expression:

You can repeat this as many times as you'd like, mixing up the physical characteristics, personality traits, and forms of gender/ creative expression for each of the genders above, and you can add more gender identities and do the same for those.

Discussion questions

1. Why do you think some people are so attached to people of a certain gender looking or acting a particular way? Whom does this benefit, if anyone, and whom does this harm, if anyone?

2. How did it feel after mixing up the representations of each gender? What are some of the potential reactions, both negative and positive, that other people have to a person who challenges societal expectations about gender?

3. What can you do to support and advocate for shifts in cultural expectations about gender and expression?

TRANSITION AND PRONOUNS AND NAMES—OH MY!
· ·

How do we define transitioning as it relates to being transgender? *We* don't! Only the individual can tell us what transitioning means to them, if anything at all. Some people would say their transition begins when they come out to themselves and ends with a specific transition-related goal, such as a legal name, pronoun, or gender marker change. Some people who take hormones might describe their transition as being lifelong since they will take them for the rest of their lives. Others would not find the term transition relevant to their experience since they always knew how they felt on the inside, regardless of how people perceived or labeled them. Since people have their own unique experiences, they will determine for themselves what feels right for them.

Read the scenarios below and describe your initial thoughts and feelings:

1. Your friend who was assumed to be male at birth comes out to you as trans.
    a. What are the first thoughts that come to your mind as it relates to your friend's transition?
    b. Did you make any assumptions? If so, what were they?
    c. She tells you that she goes by a different name, uses the pronouns she/her/hers, and is going to start taking estrogen as soon as she turns 18 next year. How would you respond to this?

2. Your cousin tells you that they feel like their gender is fluid. Sometimes they feel more like a boy, and sometimes they feel more like a girl. Sometimes they feel like neither or both at the same time. They ask you to refer to them as they/them/their.

a. If this is the first time you are using the pronouns they/them/their for someone, how does it feel to you? If you have used the pronouns they/them/their for someone in your life, think back to when you heard about it for the first time. How did it feel to you to use the singular pronouns they/them/their?

b. How do you think it felt or would feel for the person to hear someone use the correct pronouns for them?

OKTA (OK TO ASK) OR NOYB (NONE OF YOUR BUSINESS)

Have someone read each of the following statements about transgender and non-binary experience out loud. Decide whether or not you think it's OK to ask or not OK to ask a person and say out loud to yourself or collectively if in a group setting, either OKTA (OK to ask) or NOYB (None of your business):

Where do you shop for clothes?	OKTA NOYB
Do you wear boy or girl underwear?	OKTA NOYB
Do you like to play sports?	OKTA NOYB
Do you wear a jockstrap or a sports bra when you play sports?	OKTA NOYB
Which restroom do you feel most comfortable using?	OKTA NOYB
What is the name you were assigned at birth?	OKTA NOYB

Do you stand or sit down when you use the restroom?   OKTA   NOYB

What pronouns do you use?   OKTA   NOYB

Is there a name you prefer to go by?   OKTA   NOYB

What is between your legs?   OKTA   NOYB

When we think about why certain questions may be NOYB, it's important to consider the motive in asking the question. Let's look at why we want to be mindful of the NOYB questions from above:

Do you wear boy or girl underwear? It's not appropriate to ask this question if the intention is to find out what gender someone is. If you are shopping for a gift, you can ask what style, fabric, or color underwear someone likes.

Do you wear a jockstrap or a sports bra when you play sports? This is an inappropriate question because it is trying to get at something that can be very sensitive and personal to an individual.

What is the name you were assigned at birth? Even with good or curious intentions, this question is not good etiquette. The question can kick up a lot of feelings and is very private to many trans folks.

Do you stand or sit down when you use the restroom? If you are trying to ask someone if they did a #1 or a #2, that is one thing (which often is very private for some folks). It's not nice or respectful to ask this question as it is only being asked to find out the person's genitalia.

What is between your legs? IT IS NOT OK TO ASK ANY PERSON THIS QUESTION. If you are in an intimate relationship with someone and the person feels safe and comfortable disclosing private details about their body, they will let you know.

We are wired to gender people by looking at them or hearing their voice. It is ingrained in us at a very young age. Changing the way that we approach or think about people takes a bit of rewiring of the brain. One of the key ways that we can do this is through practice so that it sticks. If you have known someone to be female and have used the pronouns she/her/hers for this person, and are having difficulty using different pronouns such as he/him/his for this same person, you will need to practice! You can have all the good intentions in the world and even accept that this is a change and process for you, too. You still at some point, sooner than later, will need to get it right, right? You will show true respect, support, and affirmation of your loved one when you consistently use the correct pronouns!

You will have additional opportunities to practice in Chapter 6 and throughout the workbook.

PRONOUN PRACTICE MAKES PERFECT!

Find a picture of a person in your life for whom you are wanting to remember to use the correct pronouns. It can be a printed photo or a photo of the person on your phone or computer. Either way, keep the photo by you where you can easily glance at it. Now, take a few minutes to answer the following questions about this person, using the correct pronouns. As you are writing the responses, say them out loud while looking at the photo. This will help you to practice associating this person with the correct pronouns.

1. The important person in my life who I am working on using the correct pronouns for is _____ (name) and this important person in my life uses the pronouns _____ / _____ / _____.

2. What is one of the ways that _____ (correct pronoun) likes to have fun?

   _____

   _____

   _____

3. How did you meet _____ (correct pronoun)?

   _____

   _____

   _____

4. What is one thing you admire about _____ (correct pronoun)?

   _____

   _____

   _____

5. What is one good memory you have of you and _____ (correct pronoun)?

   _____

   _____

   _____

Now that you have practiced writing and verbally saying aloud the correct pronouns, you can practice even more in different ways! You can go in front of a mirror and answer those same questions or different questions about the person using the correct pronouns. You can continue to repeat them a few times a day, every day, until you notice that it becomes automatic. Prove to yourself and to your loved one that pronoun practice does make perfect!

THAT'S AWKWARD! SITUATION RESPONSES

Read the following scenarios and think about how you would respond in these situations:

1. You're out getting ice-cream with your friend who uses the pronouns he/him. You both order your cones and step aside to wait for your order. When your cone is ready, you go up and grab it from the worker. The worker says to you out loud in front of everyone there, "If you hold on a minute, I can give you her cone, too."

How would you respond if at all in this situation? Would you say something to the worker in private or say it in front of your friend and why?

2. You're out at the mall with your friends and someone walks past wearing a dress with a beard and lipstick on. One of your friends says to the group, "Was that a boy or a girl or...? I think that person may be confused."

How would you respond if at all in this situation? Would you say something to your friend in private or in front of the whole group and why?

When in a situation where you feel that you need to correct someone who misgenders someone or says something that may be potentially harmful to another individual or community, think about how what you will say will benefit the person you are advocating for and/or the person who made the statement and/or other people there who may have heard the potentially harmful (even if unintentionally harmful) comment. If there is a teachable moment, teach away!

Some potential responses to the worker, in private or out loud, in the ice-cream pronoun scenario:

> "Thanks! I'll let him know that his cone is almost ready so that he can grab it."

> "That's OK, my friend likes to get his own ice-cream when it's ready because he thinks I'll eat it!"

Taking an approach of just saying something back, using the correct pronoun when referring to your friend, can be very beneficial. It doesn't call out your friend as being trans or potentially embarrass them by making it into a situation.

Some potential responses to the friend, in private or to the group, in the mall "gender-fabulous" scenario:

> "I don't think that person is confused. They seemed pretty sure and happy when they walked by smiling and looking fabulous."

> "How can we know the person's gender just by looking at them? I think it's so cool when someone can be exactly who they are."

"I think the person was just expressing themself how they feel
    most comfortable. Clothing and facial hair do not imply or define
    our gender."

Responding to a friend who makes a judgmental statement about
someone for how they may express or not express their gender
using positive affirmations about the person may help your friend
to see their mistake in a way that doesn't put the emphasis on
how inappropriate or rude the comment was. Instead, the response
demonstrates your positive take on that person's gender expression
or creative expression. This is important because shaming and
blaming can potentially cause people to feel defensive and
shut down. Taking a more positive approach is encouraging and
empowering.

Transitioning is a huge umbrella with many layers and
possibilities. For some, transitioning is an important process and
part of trans experience. Some people change their name legally
while others may go by a different name and still have to use their
previous name for legal purposes. Some people will change their
gender marker from male/M to female/F or from female/F to male/M.
In some areas of the country a person can use non-binary as their
gender marker on their legal identification. A minor cannot make
legal changes to their name or gender marker without the consent
of a parent. Others may want to take hormones such as testosterone
or estrogen. Some have the desire to make changes to their bodies to
feel like their authentic selves. Others have no desire to transition by
making any changes to their name or bodies. The only thing we can
know about a person's transition is what they tell us.

THINGS TO DO...DO THOSE THINGS!

Once a friend, family member, or loved one comes out to you as being trans and confidentially tells you anything about their transition process and what it entails, that should prompt every Super Trans Ally to write a things-to-do list and then *do those things*! Depending on that person's transition experience, some of the list items may include:

1. Change the person's name in my phone.

2. Practice using the correct pronouns.

3. Take them shopping for clothes!

4. Write a letter to the school principal to advocate for all-gender restrooms.

5. Teach my friend how to put on a tie and/or give them some makeup tips.

6. Offer to help them find a trans-affirming doctor and go with them to a consult.

SNAPSHOT OF TAKE-AWAYS FROM THIS CHAPTER

There is diversity within and among gender diverse communities. There are many ways for a person to experience being trans and/or non-binary. Keep in mind that a person can be both trans and non-binary at the same time! It is a fact that we are who we say we are!

1. Not only can we not judge a book by its cover, but we also cannot judge a cover by its book! There is no right or wrong way to be a girl/woman, boy/man, neither, gender fluid, or gender fab! It can feel frustrating when we feel limited in our choices pertaining to our gender and expression because of expectations and rules about who we are supposed to be.

2. The concept of transitioning may have a different meaning for different people. Some trans people will have a goal or many goals towards reaching their transition, while others will consider transitioning a lifelong process. Some will not even relate to the word or have a desire to transition. Ask respectful questions. People will tell you what they want you to know. Respect the right to privacy. Accept that people may not want to discuss this topic.

3. When someone wants you to use a different name and pronoun to refer to them by, *use it right away*. If you make a mistake, try harder. If you make another mistake, try even harder. Practice. Practice. Practice. When something is important to us, we make time for it and we get it right sooner rather than later!

CHAPTER 5

Ask, Don't Assume

You Only Know What They Tell You

This chapter is about assumptions. We generally don't like to make assumptions but... Here's an assumption that we are willing to make: you *care* about one or more trans-identified, non-binary people, or gender diverse folks as a group. As evidence, you are reading this book! Now that we have established that you are a person who is caring, we also want to make sure that you are a person who is *careful*. That is, careful with other people's feelings and personal information.

While we want to encourage openness, curiosity, and questions, we also respect personal boundaries and recognize that it can be a drain to be put on the spot and constantly have to explain one's gender identity and/or gender expression.

Here are a few types of assumptions that will be addressed in this chapter:

- Assuming that it's OK to share someone's birth name.
- Assuming that a person wants to transition to the "opposite" gender.
- Assuming that every gender expansive person seeks medical transition such as hormones or surgery.

- Assuming it's OK to share someone's medical intervention experience (if you happen to have that information).
- Assuming someone's gender identity based on their gender expression.
- Assuming someone's sexual orientation based on their gender identity or gender expression.
- Assuming that everyone wants to answer personal questions about their gender identity.
- Assuming that people want input or advice about their physical appearance, demeanor, or voice.

CURIOSITY OR INTERROGATION?

What is the difference between being asked a question out of genuine curiosity and being grilled by a demanding inquisitor/investigator? Tone comes to mind, as well as gentleness, compassion, and respect. How can we honor the person who we are curious about? What do we actually need to know about a person? Their pronouns! It is OK to ask someone what pronouns they use so that we may refer to them in a respectful manner. Most likely, we do not need to know about another person's body.

The way a question is asked can make a difference. A young child asks your gender expansive friend or family member, "Are you a boy or a girl?" They may be genuinely curious about the person's gender and may not yet have language to describe the word "gender." They may also not know about other genders. While that question may still feel like an intrusion, it may not feel as disrespectful as a question like "What are you?" A good answer to that question is "I am a person." Or if you are using your voice to speak up on behalf of your friend or family member, you can say something like "My friend is a person."

FREQUENTLY ASKED QUESTIONS ABOUT GENDER DIVERSE FRIENDS AND FAMILY

Just because you know someone's birth name, gender assumed at birth, or medical transition information, do not assume that it's OK to share. People often ask questions like these:

- So, were they born a girl or a boy?
- What was their birth name?
- What did they do medically to transition?

While it may seem harmless to answer these questions, it creates a kind of sensationalized gossip. Why do people need such information? Will they somehow feel the person is more legitimate in their opinion? Does it create a tidy box into which the person can be placed?

RESPONDING TO UNCOMFORTABLE QUESTIONS

Often, a good answer to an uncomfortable question is a short, simple sentence. For example:

- "I'm not at liberty to say."
- "I don't know."
- "I'm not sure."
- "I'm not comfortable discussing that."
- "That's not mine to tell."
- "I'd rather not talk about it."
- "It's not our business to discuss."
- "Let's not gossip about them."
- "Let's talk about our weekend plans instead."

- "Why do you need to know?"
- "I can't share that information."

Circle one or more of the short sentences above that feels best to you. Practice saying it a few times out loud now so that you will remember to say it when needed.

Regarding medical details, you could also say, "That's private/personal information," and explain that some people opt for medical transition such as hormones or surgery and some do not. We cannot assume that every transgender person wants or has financial access to medical transition or wants to be the "opposite" gender. This assumption is based on the belief that gender is binary. Any person of any gender may subscribe to a binary system of gender. Just like some cisgender folks think there are only two genders, some trans folks also believe this. This way of thinking can often lead many who do not identify within a binary to feel invisible. We want to respect everyone's process and how they self-identify. At the same time it is OK to gently challenge this assumption and try to open other people's eyes and minds to our expansive gender universe.

Some people like to answer questions about themselves. Some do not. Some people are offended by personal questions. Do you ask your cisgender friends personal questions about their gender? Would you like to be asked personal questions about your gender identity or gender expression? Could you explain your own gender identity if you were asked? Even if you felt you could, would you want to explain it again and again to every new person that you encounter?

Unless a person has agreed to allow you to interview them about their life, it is not necessarily comfortable to be asked probing personal questions, especially about one's gender. Some questions cross the line from curiosity into interrogation. Getting to know people over time will allow a gradual unfolding of personal perspectives. Could you ask a question every now and then instead of all at one time? Could you let the person voluntarily say whatever they want to share about their gender journey? Could it be the case that you don't really *need* to know details? Let your friend or family member know you have questions and see if they would prefer if you asked them directly or found other resources. Not everyone has the time, energy, or desire to educate others or the endurance that it takes to educate everyone all the time.

ARE YOU A GOOD LISTENER?

Do you consider yourself a good listener? Are you paying attention when a person is speaking to you? Do people get frustrated with you because you are constantly distracted by your phone? Would you even know if they were frustrated? Do you practice active listening skills? What are those skills, you ask?

Can you name a few ways that you like to be heard, understood, witnessed?

1. _____

2. _____

3. _____

Generally, active listening sounds like:

- one person speaking at a time
- asking questions to help clarify understandings
- acknowledging what is being shared
- asking before offering advice.

Active listening looks like:

- engaged body language
- eye contact (keep in mind that not everyone is willing or able to make or sustain eye contact).

Active listening feels like:

- being fully seen/heard and witnessed
- being present in the moment
- positive attention
- receiving rather than judging.

When you are practicing active listening, you may hear things that you don't agree with or that don't make sense to you.

It's OK to acknowledge that this is someone's personal perspective. Acknowledgment does not mean that you agree with everything the person speaking is sharing. Saying "OK" is different from saying "I agree."

HOW DO WE CREATE SPACE FOR PEOPLE TO SHARE THEIR PERSONAL JOURNEYS WITH US?

How can we create deep relationships in which we can show up fully as ourselves and allow others to do the same? What are the ingredients in the recipe of mutual support?

What makes you feel comfortable in interactions with friends, family, or peers?

1. _____

2. _____

3. _____

What makes you feel uncomfortable in interactions with friends, family, or peers?

1. _____

2. _____

3. _____

How can you create a space in which another person feels comfortable sharing their stories and experiences with you?

1. _____

2. _____

3. _____

Some elements we value include active listening, mutual support and acceptance (a judgment-free zone), acknowledging the person's experience and perspective, and encouraging truth-telling and courageous sharing. Being brave enough to be vulnerable can feel like a risk because then the other person knows your information or feelings. It is a love offering. We hope that the person you are trusting will respond with kindness and empathy, and will respect your confidentiality.

Respecting confidentiality means that we keep people's identities and personal business secure. That means that we do not share their information with others unless we have asked and received permission. If everyone knows your trans masculine friend is Sage and you start talking in general about a trans masculine friend, people will assume that you are talking about Sage whether you mention his name or not.

If something is shared with us, we can find a way to talk about the issue from an "I" perspective. For example, "I need to learn more about the effects of taking hormones," rather than what sounds like gossip: "Casey told me that he is going to start taking T." (T = the hormone testosterone.) In the latter instance, is the person cashing in on some "cool points" for being associated with a trans person? Can we agree that it's even cooler to keep someone's confidentiality?

CONFIDENTIALITY QUICK QUIZ

Imagine a situation in which your friend shares some deeply personal information with you, such as: that they are questioning their sexual orientation or gender identity, that they are experiencing a medical or mental health challenge, that they have a learning difference or a non-visible disability, or that their parents are getting divorced. What would you do?

A. Tell other friends right away and swear them to secrecy.

B. Post supportive messages on social media.

C. Ask your friend what support they need and work with them to get them to the right resources.

Discussion

While it may be tempting to tell others, that could be considered gossip and your friend might feel betrayed. It could be beneficial to post general support on social media, but if you tag your friend to identify them, that could be uncomfortable and upsetting. We do not want to assume that the friend wants that kind of attention. The best choice is C because it lets your friend know that you care and that you want to help them to get support. By not sharing their personal and confidential information, you show that you are trustworthy.

What is the difference between keeping quiet out of shame and respecting another person's right to share if and when they are ready? There is a different feeling: shame can be based on fear which is silencing and disempowering; while respecting personal information and boundaries can feel like trusting and accepting that the person has their own timing and process. Even if we want the person to hurry up and "come out," they have a right to their pace and experience. Sometimes relatives or peers may want the person to stay in the closet and not "make waves" for fear of judgment or safety. Again, it is up to the individual when, how, and whether they "come out." As an ally, you can be there to support them if and when they are ready to share.

How do we care for our gender diverse loved one's privacy while still honoring our own need to express our experiences? Where is the line between our experience or story and our friend or family member's story? It would be amazing if everyone could be safe (physically and emotionally) to be "out" and freely reveal their personal information whenever they desired to do so. This would create a stigma-free society in which many people would realize that they know someone or multiple people who identify as gender expansive. In an ideal world, we would love everyone to feel secure and truly be safe enough to come out anywhere and everywhere. Yet trans folks are still at risk of harassment and violence, so we advocate for individual choice about when and to whom personal information is shared. Similarly, Super Trans Allies should follow this ethic: "It's not mine to tell." Outing is a no-no unless you have permission. What is yours to tell? That you care deeply about your gender diverse friends and loved ones and want what's best for them. You can have a general conversation that promotes acceptance without naming names. If you feel strongly that you need to name names, ask your trans loved one's permission first. If they say no, respect that. If they say yes, that should be assumed to be on a case-by-case basis. Revisit the question of revealing personal information as often as needed to get consent for each new situation or person.

RESPECTFUL BOUNDARIES SCENARIO

Here's an example of a brief interaction with a friend which demonstrates respectful boundaries:

Friend: Why do you care so much about trans issues? You are not trans.

You: Someone close to me is non-binary *or* I have gender expansive folks in my family.

Friend: Really?!? Who?

You: I prefer to respect their confidentiality.

Friend: Why won't you tell me? Are you ashamed or something?

You: I'm proud of my gender diverse friends and family. I just think it's their business to share about their lives when and with whom they choose.

How can you help connect people who would benefit from knowing each other while respecting confidentiality? It takes a little more effort and thoughtfulness than just blurting out names and identities. First, ask person 1 if they would be willing to speak to a friend (without naming names) who has a common interest or shares an identity. Next, ask person 2 if they would be willing to speak to a friend (without naming names) who has a common interest or shares an identity. If both people say yes, then make the introduction. If one or the other or both say no, then let go of the idea, even if you think it is the best idea in the world.

A note about exceptions to confidentiality: If you have concerns that your friend or family member is in danger of harming themself or others, or is being harmed, then you should reach out for help. It is important to be very mindful and intentional about who you connect with for help because systemic transphobia, racism, and immigration status concerns may make it complicated to report issues which require engaging with social systems such as the medical system and law enforcement. Try to identify trusted adults who will put the safety and wellbeing of your loved one first.

COMPLIMENT OR NOT?

Sometimes when we are trying to compliment someone, it comes out in a way that may be unintentionally insulting and hurtful. Each scenario below has a pair of statements that are intended to be a compliment. One of the statements is a compliment while the other is not. After you determine which one is the compliment, write in the space your own version of a compliment related to each given scenario.

"I like the dress you're wearing! You look stunning today!"

"I like the red dress you're wearing! It hides the fact that you don't have lady curves very well!"

Compliment: _____

"Your cheekbones make you too pretty to be a boy!"

"I wish I had your cheekbones! You're such a handsome boy!"

Compliment: _____

"When you cross your legs, you pass more like a woman."

"You are a woman no matter which way you choose to sit."

Compliment: _____

"I'm going to take you shopping and help you dress and look more like a boy!"

"I'm going to take you shopping so you can express your beautiful self however you want to!"

Compliment: _____

"I had no idea you were trans. You really look like a guy!"

"I like your style! You have great fashion sense!"

Compliment: _____

"You look so much more feminine without any facial hair. Keep shaving every day."

"I think your face looks good no matter how you have it. You're a beautiful person."

Compliment: _____

The statements that are insulting are also called microaggressions. They are problematic because they are insults in the disguise of a compliment. Even if it is subtle or unintentional, it still entails looking at a particular community with a negative lens. We have to pay very close attention to the compliments we give others to ensure they are, indeed, just compliments. There is nothing wrong with keeping it short and sweet. "You are an awesome Super Trans Ally!"

As human beings, we are wired to make assumptions. We have all made assumptions about other people, and we have all had assumptions made about us. Refraining from making assumptions and challenging assumptions takes work. This entails a change in the way we think. We have to be aware of when we are on automatic pilot and shift back into control of our own navigation system. We can all work on thinking before we act on our thoughts. A really important part of this process includes observing our thoughts. What led to the thought? Is the thought coming from a mind that is on autopilot? Is there another way to perceive something without preconceived notions? Think. Observe. Rethink. Act. Aim to act intentionally, thoughtfully, and compassionately. It's a good practice to have for avoiding making assumptions!

CHAPTER 6

Use Your Voice for Your Trans Sibling, Cousin, or Loved One and Help Grandma Remember

The idea of talking to Grandma represents talking to any family member. That could be Grandpa, parent(s)/guardian(s), siblings, aunts, uncles, older cousins, or a close friend of the family.

What does your Grandma mean to you? Is there a different special relative in your life? What are some of your favorite memories of your special relative? Fuzzy slippers and a cozy blanket? Warm cocoa or hot soup on a cold day? Baking cookies together? Big hugs and family stories? Have you told Grandma or your special relative how much they mean to you? Now is a great time to express your appreciation!

Write down one or more of your favorite memories about your special relative:

Is Grandma or your special relative a Super Trans Ally? Accepting of trans issues? Yes? How exciting! Not sure? Let's find out! No? Grab your Super Trans Ally cape!

First, let's check with our gender diverse loved one to see if they have either come out to Grandma or your special relative, if they have intentions of coming out to Grandma and plan to talk to her themself directly, or if they would prefer if you had a "fact-finding" conversation with her first to assess her level of understanding and acceptance. An important job for a Super Trans Ally is to figure out the best way and best time to speak up without stepping on your trans loved one's toes. Super Trans Ally priority: get your trans loved one's consent before outing them to anyone, especially family members. Your non-binary loved one may have strong feelings about privacy or they may be super open, or they may want to take it on a case-by-case basis. The more you can communicate with your gender expansive loved one, the better. Always respect their preferences and follow their lead. Ask them exactly what information they would want you to share and what they would not want you to share. Unless everyone in the family already knows, don't assume it's OK to share. Avoid making assumptions as that can cause stress and tension for you or your loved one and between the two of you.

WHO KNOWS?
· ·

Make a list of people who you wonder if your trans or non-binary loved one would be comfortable coming out to or is already out to:

1. _____   2. _____

3. _____   4. _____

5. _____   6. _____

7. _____   8. _____

9. _____   10. _____

Ask your loved one for more detailed information. Put a check mark (✓) if your trans loved one has already come out to the person. Put a plus sign (+) for a person that your trans loved one might come out to. Put an asterisk (*) if your non-binary loved one would like you to talk to the person first to assess the level of understanding and acceptance and/or to help educate. Put a minus sign (–) if they do not intend to talk to the relative and/or do not want you to talk to that relative.

Ask your trans or non-binary loved one if they would like you to help educate Grandma or your special relative before they come out to her or afterwards as a follow-up. Are they comfortable with you sharing their name, pronouns, and/or identity, or would they prefer you spoke to Grandma in general about trans issues?

ASSESS WHAT THEY KNOW

We hope that Grandma or your special relative is caring and concerned and open to learning. It may be the case that your relative grew up in a time when there was less awareness/acceptance about gender diversity and less trans visibility, or perhaps people in your community or culture are transphobic. It's good to start by asking what Grandma or your special relative already knows and to focus on love and acceptance. Maybe they have seen a movie or show featuring a trans actor or character. Do they need to understand vocabulary? Need help practicing pronouns? Space to talk about how different things seem from when they were growing up (regarding the gender binary)? Permission to make mistakes? Need to be heard and seen in their concern? Are these things you are comfortable taking on? It's OK to say no! Sometimes, professional support is needed. There are other resources such as therapists and community support groups to which you can direct them.

BUBBLE GUM: SUPPORT

If Grandma or your special relative has hurtful or hateful things to say, that can be upsetting to hear. Is there someone you can talk to about your disappointment or hurt feelings? Who are *your* support people? Are they good at keeping things confidential?

Write the names of three or more people you get support from:

1. _____

2. _____

3. _____

If you relay someone else's hurtful or hateful words to your gender expansive loved one, that may cause harm. Can you make an agreement with your trans loved one to let them know that you will share only if there is a lack of acceptance (at this time) but not the details of the conversation? Discuss with your trans loved one what you can do to protect them from constantly having to interface with transphobia, ignorance, fear, judgment, and/or misgendering. Perhaps they want to know all of the details, so that they are fully informed. Perhaps they want you to help be a buffer so they can be spared the specifics. Be as helpful as you can and stay in your truth and integrity.

Sometimes, acceptance comes with time. Perhaps Grandma or your special relative needs some time to process and then they will come to a place of unconditional love and support. Patience with their process can be helpful even if we wish they would hurry up already! They can be reminded that your trans loved one is eager to hear from them with accepting and affirming statements. Grandma or your special relative should be cautioned about expressing judgment and/or rejection of your gender fluid loved one as this can cause harm. Sometimes, people have "aggressive ignorance" which means that they refuse to learn and are insistent in their stance of not processing information. If that is the case, remind them that you love them and that you will be ready to help them understand when they are open to doing so. Ask them not to inflict their harmful attitude on your gender diverse loved one.

PREPARING YOURSELF TO TALK TO GRANDMA OR YOUR SPECIAL RELATIVE

When going into any situation that feels challenging or unpredictable, it's best to give yourself some encouraging words and visualize yourself wearing your Super Trans Ally cape!

Write three encouraging words or phrases for yourself:

1. _____

2. _____

3. _____

Remember why you love Grandma or your special relative. What did you write at the beginning of the chapter? Really feel the love. Breathe into that feeling. Open your heart. Consider all the directions the conversation could take if you discover that your Grandma or special relative is:

- fully accepting and welcomes ongoing learning
- ambivalent (mixed feelings)
- close-minded and unwilling to consider change.

Let's role-play or practice each of these possible perspectives. Role-plays can be done with one or more friends or support people, or you can record yourself (audio or video) to review your language, tone, and demeanor. Remember to look and listen with love when you consider your efforts. Reflect on and feel into how you can take care of yourself in each scenario. Jot down a few notes after you run through the role-play. If you are tempted to read the scene but not say it out loud, try it aloud anyway. It makes a difference.

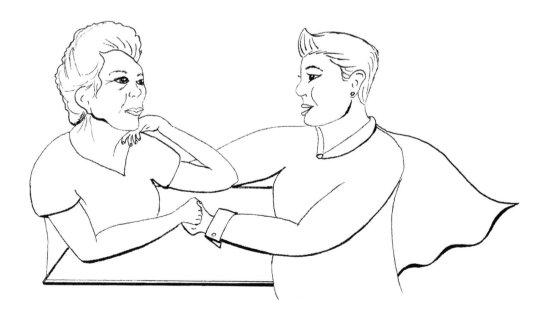

Think through all the details about how, when, and where you will have the important conversation:

- Set up a time with Grandma that will be as relaxed as possible.
- Find a quiet space such as her/their home, a restaurant or coffee shop, or a park.
- Make it happen!
- In the moment, assume good will and no prior knowledge and be open to surprises.

Feel the love flowing even if and especially if you are nervous. Breathe deeply. Trust yourself. Follow the path of the conversation to its natural conclusion. Offer follow-up such as: your continued support; videos, stories, teachings by people with lived experience; connection to community resources in person or online. Give yourself permission to make mistakes. You can always revisit the conversation another time if necessary. Do-overs are cool. Model a compassionate response and patience with yourself and with Grandma or your special relative.

After the conversation, congratulate yourself regardless of the other person's response. Give yourself a Super Trans Ally gold star. Reward yourself with something that you enjoy doing—more on that in Chapter 9!

ROLE-PLAY OPTIONS FOR VARIOUS POSSIBLE SCENARIOS (SUPPORTIVE, QUESTIONS/ CONCERNS, LESS SUPPORTIVE RESPONSE)

These role-play scenarios are intended to get you thinking about a set of possible responses. Do not feel that you should memorize the lines word for word! If you want to write in your own responses or set of talking points you would like to make, please do!

What if Grandma or your special relative cries or has a strong emotional response?

It is possible that you or Grandma may have strong emotional responses to a conversation or role-play about your non-binary loved one. How will you respond if that happens? How will you feel? Are you prepared for that? Can you allow that? Bring a few tissues with you just in case. If Grandma or your special relative has a strong reaction, it is not your responsibility to fix. Can you hold a space of love and compassion with neutrality? Getting our feelings out is healthy. It's just a question of when and with whom. If you are uncomfortable with the emotional response, what could you say or do to excuse yourself gracefully? Perhaps you could say, "I need some time to myself right now." Give yourself some space to regroup. It's OK to step away and come back later.

On the other hand, what if there is no response? Can you allow that? Perhaps revisit the idea another time to follow up.

Whatever happens, remember that you are not alone. Super Trans Allies are cheering you on. Thank you for your efforts.

Supportive response role-play

You: Grandma, do you know anyone who is transgender?

Grandma: Yes, our gender expansive relative! I've been working on educating myself.

You: Great! Tell me what you know. Let's make a plan to help educate others in the family!

Grandma: Yes! I'm open to making a plan.

You: Are you familiar with our trans loved one's name and pronouns? Is it OK with you if we practice using them? I'll be helping you to remember to use the correct name and pronouns because it makes a difference. (See "Pronoun Practice with Grandma" at the end of this chapter.)

Your notes:

_____

_____

_____

Questions and concerns role-play

You: Grandma, do you know anyone who is transgender?

Grandma: Yes, our loved one. I worry about them.

You: Grandma, what are your concerns or fears?

Grandma: That my grandchild will be bullied, excluded, harmed, and have a difficult time in life.

You: Grandma, we can't control everything, but we can express our love and full acceptance of our trans loved one. Our support creates a kind of buffer so that our loved one knows that we will be there for them, no matter what.

Grandma: Isn't this just a phase? They made this up after looking at the internet.

You: Grandma, it's super important for us to accept our gender expansive loved one. That means that we honor their identity. We have to trust that they know best how they feel. Let's think through the language that we use so we can be respectful. Telling someone that they are going through a phase is not useful. We want to validate and celebrate our trans loved one. Looking at the internet does not cause someone to identify as gender diverse. They may have discovered language to express what they were feeling and maybe they found a supportive community online.

Grandma: Can't they change back? What if they have regrets?

You: We have to trust that our genderqueer loved one is making this change because it is necessary for them to truly live. We want them to live their best life and to be fully who they are. We can't predict the future. Let's live in the present moment and care about our loved one just as they are. It is unlikely that they will have regrets about living in alignment with their gender identity so they can be themself. If they do have regrets, we will be there to support them, just as we would through any life change or challenge.

Grandma: How am I going to act around my trans grandchild?

You: You are going to act with love, as always.

Grandma: What will I tell my friends?

You: You are going to tell your friends and our family that you love your grandchild unconditionally and that you accept them. You can be an ally by educating yourself, your friends, and our family. Don't hesitate to share that you have a trans grandchild. It's important that you practice being open and honest with your friends. They may have questions or judgments. They may or may not want to talk about it. I'm here for you if you want to talk through how to approach a friend's response.

Grandma: Thank you, sweetheart.

Your notes:

Less supportive response role-play

You: Grandma, do you know anyone who is transgender?

Grandma: Yes, our loved one. I'm not comfortable using this new name and different pronouns. What's wrong with the old way? Why can't I use the name that I have been calling my loved one all these years?

You: Grandma, life is full of changes. We have an opportunity to really make a difference by supporting our gender expansive loved one by using the name and pronouns that are in alignment with their gender identity. If we are not accepting, we risk isolating our trans loved one and having an estranged relationship or no relationship with them. Is refusing to be accepting worth the risk?

Grandma: What happens if I don't stop using the birth name?

You: Grandma, let's see if we can use the analogy of a friend who got married and changed her last name. Did you ever have that experience? Did you change your last name when you got married? Were you excited to change your last name? Did your new name represent something special to you about how your life had changed? Did you want people to use your new last name? Did you have feelings when friends or family called you by your pre-marriage last name? Did you correct them? Did someone else correct them? Did they correct themselves? Did you forgive them because mistakes can happen? Did you ever call a friend by her pre-marriage last name? Did you realize your error and correct yourself out loud? Did you have feelings about that? Did you resolve to remember your friend's new last name and use it in the future? Can we do that for our trans loved one?

Grandma: I understand the point you are trying to make. I will think about it.

You: Thank you, Grandma. Let's talk again soon.

Your notes:

_____

_____

_____

"HOW SHOULD I REACT WHEN I MESS UP?" ROLE-PLAYS ABOUT GRANDMA SPEAKING TO YOUR GENDER DIVERSE LOVED ONE

Sometimes, people feel stuck when they think about being embarrassed by saying the wrong pronouns, hesitating when using different pronouns, or accidentally saying a birth name. Let's think about a few response options to the question of "How should I respond if I mess up?" See which option appeals to you most. We can role-play each one.

- A. Why can't I just call you by the name I've always called you?

- B. Thank you for correcting me.

- C. I can't remember this stuff because I don't want you to change.

- D. (Trigger warning) I will not use that name.

You can say to Grandma: "I'll play the role of Grandma (G). Grandma, you play the role of the role of our trans loved one (TLO)."

A. Why can't I just call you by the name I've always called you?

TLO: Hi, Grandma!

G: Hi, darling. How are you?

TLO: I had a good day at school until a classmate started calling me by my birth name.

G: Well, _____ (birth name), you shouldn't be surprised. That *is* your name. Why do you have to make such a fuss? What's wrong with your birth name?

TLO: I'm going to go play some video games now, Grandma.

B. Thank you for correcting me.

TLO: Hi, Grandma!

G: Hi, _____ (birth name). How are you?

TLO: Grandma, please call me _____ (current name).

G: Thank you for correcting me, _____ (current name). I'm working on getting it right. I appreciate your patience with me. You know I love you.

TLO: Thanks, Grandma. I love you, too. Let's bake those cookies now.

C. I can't remember this stuff because I don't want you to change.

TLO: Hi, Grandma!

G: Hi, _____ (birth name). How are you?

TLO: Grandma, please call me _____ (current name).

G: I can't remember all this stuff because I don't want you to change. I like your birth name. It's such a beautiful name. I have such fond memories of when you were born and when you were little. I don't want to give that up. I don't know who you are now or how I'll relate to you. You are not the same person. I can't let go of the baby and child I love.

TLO: Grandma, you don't have to let go of those memories. I am still your grandchild. I know that change can be challenging. I want us to find a way to build a new relationship based on respect. That means it's important to use my current name and pronouns. I hope that you can understand how meaningful this is to me. Your support would mean the world to me.

G: Yes, _____ (current name). I want to continue to have a relationship with you. I will work on showing you respect by using your current name and pronouns. I hope you will forgive me if I slip up.

TLO: Thank you, Grandma. I hope that I'll forgive you, too! (Both laugh and hug.)

D. (Trigger warning) I will not use that name.

TLO: Hi, Grandma!

G: Hi, _____ (birth name). How are you?

TLO: Grandma, please call me _____ (current name).

G: _____ (birth name), I will not call you by any other name.

TLO: Grandma, I feel sad when I hear you say that. It hurts my feelings. Please respect me by using my current name and pronouns.

G: I will not support your "choice" of this "lifestyle," _____ (birth name).

TLO: I hope that you will reconsider your position, Grandma. I would like to continue to have a relationship with you. I won't feel comfortable or welcome here unless I know you respect me and that includes using my current name and pronouns.

G: That's your choice.

TLO: Grandma, I'd like to check back with you another time. Can we make a date to do that?

G: All right. Let's talk in a week.

TLO: OK, Grandma. Please remember that I love you and that you love me. I hope you can find it in your heart to rise above judgment and fear so we can continue our relationship.

DEBRIEFING WITH GRANDMA

How did each of those role-play scenarios go for you? Ask Grandma how she felt about each one. Ask her which of the scenarios is closest to her own perspective. Is there another perspective that is closer to her own which was not represented? If so, ask her to talk about it and play it out.

The last situation is really challenging and can bring up many feelings. We hope that you and your trans loved one do not have to encounter such overt transphobia. Since it is a possibility, we couldn't shy away from it. When judgments and fears are present and brought to light, it can be an opportunity for healing. There is a difference between ignorance based on a lack of information and/or learned bias compared to deep-seated hate. We truly hope that as a Super Trans Ally you will be able to help educate Grandma and work around any road blocks in her path to understanding and acceptance. Should you find that there is no budging her transphobia, it may be necessary for you and/or your trans loved one to call in professional help and/or have healthy boundaries with the relationship. For some people, part of your self-care may include taking some space from someone who is hurting you. You have every right to consider taking a break if you need one.

PRONOUN PRACTICE WITH GRANDMA!

You: Grandma, let's practice using our trans loved one's pronouns! Can we have a conversation where we refer to our genderqueer loved one in the third person so we can use their correct pronouns? Pronouns may have felt automatic in the past. The change may require a little getting used to now. Grandma, I want to make sure you are not hesitating and fumbling over your words the next time we see our non-binary loved one. Sound like a plan? Let's try it!

How about a situation where your trans loved one (TLO) goes to the store to buy some groceries? You may want to pass the book to Grandma for her to fill in the blanks or circle the pronouns before speaking this situation out loud. Practice saying this a few times until it becomes automatic. Then make up a situation of your own!

Mom said that she asked _____ (TLO's name) to go to the store to buy her some groceries. Mom said ___ she/he/they/etc. (TLO's pronoun) was/were busy with homework and she had to ask ___ her/him/them/etc. (TLO's pronoun) twice. Mom said that ___ she/he/they/etc. (TLO's pronoun) has/have a big presentation for ____ her/his/their/etc. (TLO's pronoun) history class. When _____ (TLO's name) was shopping, ___ she/he/they/etc. (TLO's pronoun) set a few things on the counter and then had to walk away to pick up one more item. Another customer came to the register in the meantime and the cashier referenced your _____ sister/brother/sibling/cousin/friend/grandchild (TLO's relationship to you) and said that those items were ____ hers/his/theirs/etc. (TLO's pronoun).

How did that go for you? For Grandma? Slightly hesitant the first time and then more fluid with practice? Good job!

Write your own scenario for practice on the next page. Run it through several times with Grandma. Be sure to write the situation so that there are various forms of pronouns expressed. Sample pronouns: she/her/hers; he/him/his; they/them/their(s); write in:

--.

When you remind Grandma, your parent(s)/guardian(s), your siblings, extended family, or friends of the family to use your gender diverse loved one's pronouns or current name, do it with as much love and kindness as you can offer. We suspect that you will need to exercise patience and compassion and that it will eventually pay off even if there is a less-than-supportive response initially. If there is a hostile, unyielding response, please seek support.

Thank you so much for your Super Trans Ally efforts with Grandma, your parent(s)/guardian(s), your siblings, cousins, aunts, uncles, close family friends, or other special relative(s). We appreciate all that you do! Know that your energies and devotion make a difference. Whatever your relative's response is/was, know that your conversations or role-plays demonstrate your caring and help build acceptance and inclusion. Write an entry in the action chart in Chapter 9 and give yourself a star. We are proud of you!

CHAPTER 7

Care Beyond a Pinky Swear

Along your journey as a Super Trans Ally, you will likely come across many situations where you want to support your trans, non-binary, and gender-fabulous friends. You may even want to fly above and beyond making a supportive and affirming statement to taking more thoughtfully planned-out action to advocate with your trans friend or the community at large. One of the most important parts of making a commitment to someone you care about is following through on it. Doing what you said you would do tells your trans friend that you are committed to being a consistent and strong support to them. It also demonstrates that you wholeheartedly care *beyond* a pinky swear! As much as you might want to do everything you can think of to be the best ally you can possibly be, it's necessary to learn first what your trans and non-binary friend(s) and community need before you commit to supporting them in any particular way. You may think you know what is best for your friend, but truly only that person can tell you what support they need. Not everyone has the energy to explain to an ally what they need and how to best be of service. As a trans ally, it would be a great idea to do your own research and have some ideas about what might be useful action. More ally action ideas will be offered in Chapters 8 and 9.

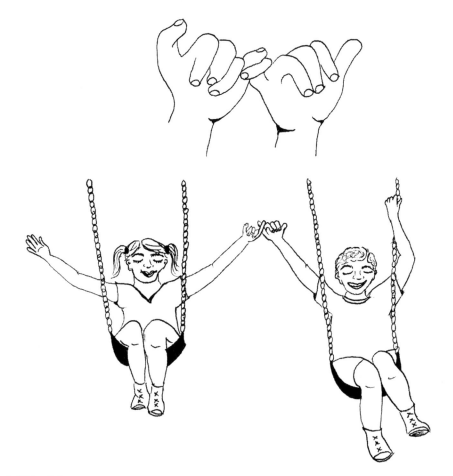

ASK–GET–GIVE

It's hard to ask for something from someone, such as support. It's also hard to remind someone who we've asked for help to remember to do it and to keep following up until they do it. Sometimes it may feel as if we are asking too much of a person or that the person is too busy, so why bother asking? This activity will help us to master the art of ask-get-give. It starts with the ASK. We ASK our loved one what they need from us, if anything. What is one thing that would be helpful, supportive, affirming, empowering, etc.? Once you ask, give them time to identify a need/ask. Once you GET the need, you can then determine what and how you are going to address it! Here is how it will go:

1. ASK: Identify the person's need. "What, if anything, can I do to support you during this time? Is there something I can do to be a better advocate for you and other trans and non-binary people?"

2. GET: Wait until you get a response from the person with a specific or general need they may have. Check in with them to see if they have new needs or if their needs have changed.

3. GIVE: Meet their need! Commit to following through with supporting them in the way that they need. Go, Super Trans Ally, go! YOU ROCK!

Identify and implement at least one ask–get–give for a trans, non-binary, or gender expansive person in your life. Check out Chapter 9 to see the chart where you can track your Super Trans Ally actions!

TOO YOUNG?

One of the things that your trans and non-binary friends may need your support around is when adults tell them that they are "too young" to feel a certain way or do something. Have you ever been told that you are "too young" to feel or know something about yourself or to make a particular decision that affects your life? For each statement below, circle whether you are too young or not too young for each experience:

Watch horror movies that are rated R	Too young	Not too young
Feel scared to not perform well on a test	Too young	Not too young
Daydream	Too young	Not too young
Feel peer pressure	Too young	Not too young
Make decisions	Too young	Not too young
Choose my friends	Too young	Not too young
Care about my friends	Too young	Not too young
Have a celebrity crush	Too young	Not too young
Have a crush on someone in real life	Too young	Not too young
Be physically attracted to someone	Too young	Not too young
Have my feelings hurt	Too young	Not too young
Play video games with violence in them	Too young	Not too young
Clean the house	Too young	Not too young
Babysit my younger siblings	Too young	Not too young
Cry when I am hurt	Too young	Not too young
Cook dinner	Too young	Not too young

Feel uncomfortable in my skin	Too young	Not too young
Swing on the playground	Too young	Not too young
Read the news	Too young	Not too young
Have an opinion	Too young	Not too young
Join a high school rock band	Too young	Not too young
Play with dolls	Too young	Not too young
Collect coins	Too young	Not too young
March for social justice	Too young	Not too young
Be emotionally attracted to someone	Too young	Not too young
Be romantically attracted to someone	Too young	Not too young
Know my sexual orientation	Too young	Not too young
Know my gender identity	Too young	Not too young
Go on a date with someone in my age group	Too young	Not too young
Know how I feel most comfortable expressing my gender	Too young	Not too young
Know how I feel most comfortable expressing myself	Too young	Not too young

If you have ever been told that you are too young to experience any of the things above, how did it make you feel? If you haven't been told you are too young to experience these things, how would it make you feel if you were told this? Write your response here or share it if you are in a group.

It's invalidating when people tell you that you couldn't possibly know your own feelings. For some, it can make them feel disempowered or angry and frustrated when this happens. Trans and non-binary youth often hear that they are too young to know their own gender! Parent(s), relatives, and "professionals" at school or in the community may say, "It's just a phase." Eating only vanilla ice-cream or wearing the color purple every day may just be a phase. Stating that your gender is different from the one you were thought to be when you were born is not a phase. For some people, their gender may be fluid, but only the individual can tell the rest of the world how they identify their gender at any given moment. It can be extremely difficult for a trans and/or non-binary person to hear someone say, "It is just a phase." How can you as a Super Trans Ally be supportive and affirming to a friend getting this message from relatives and community?

FROM AGEISM TO EMPOWERMENT
. . . .

This is a role-playing activity you can do with your trans, non-binary, and gender expansive friends and loved ones to help them practice and better prepare for having sometimes very personal and tough conversations with adults who question their feelings and choices. Read the ageist statements below. Your trans friend can feel free to use the possible responses provided below if it's helpful in formulating their own response. These are very personal and sometimes sensitive questions that take time and trust to open up and share.

Statements:

1. You can't know at this age that your gender is different from the one you were "born with."

2. Wait until you are 18 and an adult to see how you feel and make a decision then.

3. You're too young to have a romantic or sexual attraction to someone of the same gender. It's just a phase.

Possible responses to the statements:

1. I can know because it's my body. It's my heart. It's my mind. This is my truth. It's a feeling and something that only I can know and I will always know at any given moment what feels right to me. I need you to believe in me, support me, and love me unconditionally.
    a. I may have been given that gender when I was born, but I do not identify as that gender. I know that I am a different gender.

2. I make a lot of decisions at my age.
   a. For example, I decided that I was going to study hard and get good grades so that I can get into a good college.
   b. For example, I decided that I could go to school and work a part-time job.
   c. For example, I decided not to drink underage and not to let peer pressure get to me.
   d. I am certain that I am able to know how I feel at this age, and to make decisions about who I am and how I want to express myself.
   e. Please respect that I am an intelligent, creative, ambitious, hard-working young person who makes thoughtful and intentional choices that impact my life and wellbeing.

3. The truth is that I know my own heart and I can have feelings and attractions at my age. It may be hard for you to hear, but this is my reality. I am attracted to people of the same gender.

Perhaps this activity can challenge adults to rethink their approach and perspectives on the topic. You can also remind your trans friend that they know themself and no one else can tell them who they are or how they feel. Empower your friend to not allow age discrimination or a proclaimed desire from a loved one to "protect" them make them doubt their feelings, experiences, and decisions. They have every right to feel validated and to prioritize their own wellbeing.

While on the topic of emotional wellness, it is important to note that prejudice, transphobia, and discrimination against trans, non-binary, and gender diverse people is a reality for many, and these experiences can take a toll on a person's emotional wellbeing over time. Being trans and non-binary is not a mental illness. As is true for every community across all identities, some trans and non-binary folks live with a range of mental health issues, while others do not. Sometimes a trans person's mental health issues may be triggered by a negative experience or experiences of discrimination related to their gender identity and expression. With this being said, not every trans and non-binary person experiences discrimination and hatred for being trans. Not all trans people have had a horrific trans-related experience. Many trans people have positive experiences on their gender journey.

There may also be challenges and real fears that are associated with being out and with the anticipation of being the target of some form of discrimination. A lot of trans and non-binary folks are very proud of who they are and their gender identity. Many trans and non-binary folks are extremely resilient and courageous. Do not assume that just because a person is trans that they are currently suffering or will inevitably suffer. Trans people can and do live very happy, healthy, and productive lives. With that said, regardless of where you think or know your trans friend or family member is on the emotional wellness spectrum, the reality still remains that trans youth are at higher risk for making suicide attempts than their LGB and straight peers, and, therefore, it is always a good idea as a Super Trans Ally to check in with your gender diverse friends regularly to see how they are doing in general.

You are rocking at being a Super Trans Ally! Even with all of your support, there are going to be people who can and may hurt your gender expansive friends. They may be strangers or family, friends, and other people close to your friend who say things and do things that can be potentially hurtful and harmful. Although you can't prevent them from ever getting hurt, you can be there afterwards and you can also help them to be proactive and to identify positive and even creative outlets for any real or anticipated situations that have caused or may cause hurt in the future.

DISMISS IT (POETRY/SPOKEN WORD/SONGWRITING)

Use any or all of the words/phrases given to write poetry. This can be a solo activity or a group activity. If in a group, you can split up into smaller groups and each collectively write and perform your spoken word pieces. (An alternative to writing poetry is to just free-write using one or more of the words/phrases below, or you can opt to use any or all of the words/phrases to write an original song!)

Words/phrases to choose from

- Just a phase
- Too young
- I know myself
- My body
- My mind
- Parental consent
- Support
- Discrimination
- Dismiss
- Don't judge me
- Judgmental
- Assumptions
- My truth
- My life
- Understand
- Accept me
- Who I am
- Strong
- A voice

Now add your own words/phrases/lyrics!

EMPATHY AND SYMPATHY: WHAT'S THE DIFFERENCE?

Part of being a friend in general is caring when your friend is experiencing pain, suffering, or any type of difficult time in their life. Sympathy is feeling sorry for someone. Empathy is having an understanding of what someone might be going through and recognizing their feelings. Do we need to have had exactly the same experience as someone else in order to put ourselves in their shoes? Can we use our own life experiences to recognize the challenges that someone else is going through without feeling sorry for them? Let's explore this idea in our next activity.

SWEAT OR SWEET?

We all have been in situations where we may feel a bit uncomfortable. When we have the option to not be in those situations, we can opt out. There are some situations where it may not be as simple as opting out. Some situations can be more than just a bit stressful for trans and non-binary folks. It can cause a great deal of anxiety to be in the situation or even just to anticipate being in the situation. In an effort to help us all understand the impact a stressful situation can have on a person, we will try the approach of naming it and relating to it. Rather than feeling sorry for the person's pain or discomfort, we will first hear the person label the impact, and then we can relate to and understand it better.

For any situation below that isn't hard for you or is neutral and you don't really think twice about, circle "Sweet." For any situation that makes you feel uneasy, uncomfortable, stressed, and/or anxious, circle "Sweat." If you circle "Sweet" for a situation, identify in the space below each scenario what you think might be challenging for someone else who may circle "Sweat" for that same situation. If you are doing this activity in a group setting, pair up and each of you pick one example you selected "Sweat" for and talk about why you chose it and your feelings about the situation.

Driving or biking   Sweet   Sweat

Quizzes, tests, and exams   Sweet   Sweat

Public restrooms (not single-stall)   Sweet   Sweat

Going to school   Sweet   Sweat

Gym locker room   Sweet   Sweat

School dance   Sweet   Sweat

First day of school or camp   Sweet   Sweat

Doctor's office   Sweet   Sweat

Having a crush   Sweet   Sweat

Going on a date   Sweet   Sweat

Being with family (parent(s)/guardian(s)/sibling(s))   Sweet   Sweat

----

Interacting with extended relatives   Sweet Sweat

Spending time with friends   Sweet Sweat

Airport security   Sweet Sweat

Clothes shopping   Sweet Sweat

Fitting room in clothing stores   Sweet Sweat

Being misgendered (referred to using incorrect Sweet Sweat
pronoun)

Some of the things that cisgender people may take for granted are things that may increase stress and discomfort among trans and non-binary folks. This is called cisgender privilege. While cisgender and transgender young people may circle "Sweat" for some of the same things listed above, there may be different reasons for this. What are some experiences that a trans person may have that a cisgender person may not experience in some of those situations listed? Even among trans people there are folks who also belong to other marginalized identities including people of color and people with disabilities. Trans white people experience white privilege and some trans males may experience male privilege. People who are trans and belong to other marginalized identities may experience mistreatment based on more than one part of their identity. It's important to be mindful of this as an ally.

DO NOTHING/SAY SOMETHING/GO BEYOND

Sometimes, even though you have great intentions, you may feel as if you don't have it in you at the time to say or do anything to support a trans friend or loved one in the moment. You may observe someone making a disrespectful comment or joke about trans people and not want to say something or feel uncomfortable saying something. That is always your right. But you can say something if you feel safe doing so, even if it means stepping outside of your Comfort Zone and into your Courage Zone. Here are some scenarios that may come up where you may have to make a decision to do nothing or do something. What might you do in these situations? Do nothing or do something? If you would do something, what would you do? Some examples are provided below.

Scenario: You are with a group in the hallway at your school and one of the students makes a disrespectful statement about trans people, stating that they shouldn't have "special" rights such as having access to an all-gender restroom.

Do nothing/Say something

Say something:

Example of saying something:

> "That's really not OK to say. Trans people aren't asking for 'special' rights, just equal rights and access to a restroom where they can feel safe going. Have you ever been scared or worried about using a public bathroom? We all have the same mission when we go in and we all deserve to accomplish that mission in peace."

Scenario: You are talking to a friend about your non-binary friend who uses the pronouns they/them. Your friend uses the incorrect pronouns he/him when referring to your mutual non-binary friend. You correct the person and the friend still refuses to use they/them, stating that it doesn't make sense and that it doesn't matter.

Do nothing/Say something

Say something:

Example of saying something:

> "I think it matters because our friend needs our support. They are going to cross paths with so many people who will not support them and refuse to use their correct pronouns. That's why it will mean so much for them to have two good friends who care enough to make the effort to validate and accept them for who they are. Please join me in making every effort we can to be here for our friend. Thanks!"

You can be a good friend by saying something in these situations if you feel safe doing so. You can provide supportive and encouraging words to your trans and non-binary friends when they need it. You can also show them that you're committed to being an advocate and an ally. Being a Super Trans Ally may take more of your time and energy, and of course it is a great use of your time and energy! As an example, your trans friend may feel stressed about having to use a public gendered restroom. You may offer to walk your friend to the bathroom and stand at the door if that is something they wish to have you do to help them feel safe. As a Super Trans Ally, you can take steps above and beyond supporting your friend this one time, and become an advocate for change at that facility. Whether it is a gendered restroom at school, a restaurant, a doctor's office, or anywhere else public, you can advocate for an all-gender restroom. Here are some potential steps you can take:

1. Ask to speak with a manager or school official such as a principal.

2. Communicate what the issue is and the importance of having an all-gender restroom (i.e. safety, inclusion, the health issue of trans people holding it in all day, etc.).

3. Give them potential alternatives such as allocating at least one restroom for all genders, whether single-stall or multi-stall. Also, having all-gender restroom signage for all single-stall restrooms so any person of any gender knows they can use it.

4. Provide the employee/staff with resources. Have a pamphlet or something in writing to offer.

5. If the employee/staff is not receptive to the idea, you can consider coordinating a petition or a protest to promote inclusive practices and encourage them to reconsider having at least one all-gender restroom.

Here are three scenarios to consider how you can be a support and how you can go above and beyond to advocate for your gender diverse friends. Read each situation below and describe how you can be a supportive friend as well as what steps you can take to go above and beyond as a Super Trans Ally!

Scenario 1: Supporting a trans and/or non-binary friend around the school dress code if there is no policy for allowing trans students to use the dress code aligned with the gender they identify as.

Supportive statement(s):

Be a Super Trans Ally and take steps to advocate for change:

1. _____

2. _____

3. _____

4. _____

5. _____

Scenario 2: Supporting and advocating for having trans bodies, experiences, sexual health, and relationships included in the general health class at school. Consider how schools separate people into gender binary classes and where non-binary people go.

Supportive statement(s):

_____

_____

_____

Be a Super Trans Ally and take steps to advocate for change:

1. _____

2. _____

3. _____

4. _____

5. _____

Scenario 3: Supporting events that celebrate, empower, and are inclusive of trans, non-binary, and gender expansive communities such as Pride, Trans Day of Remembrance, International Trans Day of Visibility, and Trans Wellness Conferences.

Supportive statement(s):

_____

_____

_____

Be a Super Trans Ally and take steps to advocate for change:

1. _____

2. _____

3. _____

4. _____

5. _____

BUBBLE GUM: EMPOWER

We strive to speak our truth, stand our ground, and share our lived experience and knowledge with others. In some cases, people do not do anything because they think it won't make any difference. The truth is that being just one person who says or does something to make a difference can change and even save a person's life! Even if you try to advocate for changing a policy or system to be more inclusive of gender diverse people and nothing changes, you have set the wheels in motion. You have also shown your trans friends and family members that their life and wellbeing matters to you. That could mean the world to them. It doesn't change the fact that it's frustrating and can feel disempowering when you put all of your effort into something and it doesn't change. Empowerment comes from communication, collaboration, and momentum. What are the benefits of your efforts? What are you learning? What can be built on the foundation you are organizing/creating? What can you do to channel your energy when you feel defeated or disempowered or just frustrated?

MOVING THROUGH FRUSTRATION

Here are some ideas to get you started:

- Practice self-care.
- Breathe deeply and mindfully.
- Disconnect from negative, toxic energies.
- Connect with nature.
- Express your frustration and disappointment at injustice and

do not direct those energies inward. It is not your fault! Please do not blame yourself or speak harshly to yourself.

- Try healthy things that can get the anger out. Punch a punching bag. Scream into a pillow. Get it out of your system! Dance it out!
- Channel your anger: protest, keep on organizing, keep on connecting.
- Create an educational opportunity with media!
- Crumple up paper.
- Stomp.
- Shake it out (shake your hands, feet, head, body).
- Get a group of people together to let it out physically. Or talk it out and support each other.
- Recognize that you are doing the best you can and forces that may be beyond your control are at play. Your efforts matter and make a difference. Remember that! Even though we may want the world to change now, it may be a process. Every step and effort along the way counts!

What other ideas do you have for showing you care beyond a pinky swear?

CHAPTER 8

Now You're the Teacher: School Everyone

This chapter will empower and encourage you to teach everyone what you know as a Super Trans Ally. We come into contact with many people in our travels such as neighbors and cashiers at grocery stores, coffee shops, or clothing stores, and other patrons of those stores. We may see bus drivers or other transportation workers, restaurant service workers, health care workers, postal workers or other government agents, and if we are employed, we interact with people at our jobs. As our emphasis is on youth empowerment, we will focus on the experience of students who have daily interactions with other students, teachers, and administrators in schools. If you happen to be employed, advocacy in the workplace can translate as students = co-workers; teachers = managers; administration = the company.

As a Super Trans Ally, you have the opportunity to help educate everyone. One of the best things about teaching is getting to witness the "aha!" moment when something clicks for the learner. So cool! Another awesome aspect of education is figuring out a new way to help someone understand and the feeling of accomplishment at a well-described concept. There is also the joy of being appreciated as someone who helps others.

GREAT EDUCATORS

• •

Do you have any favorite teachers? Name them! Teachers are everywhere, not just in classrooms.

1. _____

2. _____

3. _____

What made them so memorable? What are some of your favorite characteristics of great teachers?

1. _____

2. _____

3. _____

We can think of a few traits we love that may also be on your list:

- Kind
- Patient
- Caring
- Calm
- Friendly
- Explains things well
- Engaging
- Enthusiastic
- Knowledgeable

- Helpful
- Humorous
- Storyteller
- Listens attentively
- Captures our imagination
- Generates excitement for learning
- Does not patronize or talk down to learner(s)
- Crafts experiences that allow learners to make meaning for themselves

Do you identify with any of these characteristics? If so, put an asterisk (*) next to that item.

Are you thinking, "What if I don't identify with any of those traits? How can I possibly teach others?" Well, being a Super Trans Ally can take many forms. Educating people is one especially useful action. Teaching can happen in social situations with groups of people or in personal interactions with individuals. Sharing what you know can happen online, verbally, or through letter writing. You do not need to have intentions of going into a teaching career just because you are helping to educate people. But if you feel happy helping people to learn, you might want to consider becoming an educator!

How do we go about teaching others? Don't teachers need to go to school for a long time? Well, yes, but we are talking about helping others understand how to be inclusive and accepting, not making you responsible for the wellbeing and learning of a group of students. So the credential that matters here is that you care. It is also important to know your subject matter, so we absolutely want to encourage you to learn as much as you can. The best teachers are lifelong learners. There is always more to learn!

What is cultural humility? It's another way to say "be humble" and avoid making assumptions when it comes to someone else's experience and culture. Let's think about where we live as an example. If you grew up in a city, would you know what it was like to grow up in a rural area? If you grew up in a suburb, would you know what living in a city was like without having experienced it firsthand? Knowing one experience does not equate to understanding another experience. Even if you happen to live in the same city as a peer, one neighborhood within a city is different from another neighborhood. There are various communities and various cultures which are often shaped by economics and race. There is a history of separation which means that communities can exist alongside one another without engaging with each other. Let's hold on to this idea of not assuming that everyone has the same experience as we do and apply it to gender.

If you identify as transgender, genderqueer, gender expansive, non-binary, Two Spirit, or with any other gender diverse identity, you are part of a group that has lived experience of relating to an unsupportive gender binary system. Yet just because you identify one way does not mean that you understand or can speak for a different experience within your own culture. For example, a trans man does not necessarily understand a non-binary identity or experience and vice versa. Even within a particular identity, race and social class create different sets of experiences. A Black trans woman is likely to experience racism in addition to sexism and transphobia/cis-sexism where a white trans woman in a society with white privilege will not usually face the burden of bigotry and discrimination by race, even though she still navigates sexism and transphobia/cis-sexism. It is important not to generalize. If you are not part of the culture, it is even more important for you to recognize that caring is different from lived experience. Learn from people with lived experience. Uplift gender diverse voices. Do not presume to speak for a community or culture that is not your own. Allies who are educators bring injustices to light to help remedy those inequalities. That can and must be done in a way that respects the range of experiences in gender expansive communities.

When you are educating others, it is best to take a respectful tone and assume no prior knowledge. Avoid sarcasm and be as direct and kind as possible. For example, perhaps someone says "transgendered" instead of "transgender." You can simply say, "The preferred language is transgender." If the person looks puzzled, you can try saying it another way, explain more, or give a different perspective.

In this case, you could say "The 'ed' on the end makes it sound past tense. Gender identity is about how one feels in the current moment." Stay empowered and try not to get embroiled in a debate.

BUBBLE GUM: EDUCATE

You are under no obligation to educate others. There are times when it may be unsafe to do so; then the best option would be to walk away. But please know that one heartfelt conversation really can make a difference. You have the power to help someone or many people to see things from a different perspective. Maybe they don't want to see things differently because they like the way things are for them now (and if they are comfortable, isn't everyone feeling the same way?). Maybe they are scared about what changing their thinking will mean. Maybe learning about the world beyond the gender binary will cause them to question their own gender and/or why gender is so strongly enforced socially.

So why do we think it helps to have difficult conversations? Because that's how we grow. We learn about ourselves and we learn about others. It matters that we continue to try. If we shut down or stop trying to connect with heart, that creates divides. We want to create bridges. We want to expand people's thinking and capacity to love. We believe in this process. We want you to believe in yourself and your power and your voice and your ability to stand up and speak up and make a difference in the world. It matters. It matters deeply. You matter. Your efforts mean a great deal to the world. We are encouraged by each other's efforts. Keep at it!

How can you as a Super Trans Ally encourage others to step outside of their comfort zone into their Courage Zone?

EN/COURAGE ZONE
· ·

For this activity, Zone 1 is the Comfort Zone. This is the zone where you are going about your day, minding your business, and not noticing or responding to anything that doesn't seem to affect you personally. Zone 2 is the Discomfort Zone. This is the zone where you notice that something was said or done that made you feel uneasy. It may not be something that directly affects you, but you start to question your role in the situation and whether you should say or do something. Zone 3 is the Courage Zone. This is the zone where you step up, use your voice, and take action in a sometimes uncomfortable situation to support a trans person in your life. This is the zone where you challenge yourself to be a brave Super Trans Ally! For each scenario below match the three responses with the zone you think the person is in.

Scenario 1

You're with a group of students on a school trip to a local museum. One of your gay cisgender friends says in front of the whole group, including your trans friend, "I don't understand trans people who say they are gay. I mean, I am gay, so I like certain body parts. They could just keep it easy and stay straight instead of changing their gender and sexual orientation."

> **Response 1:** You don't want to start any drama so you avoid responding and say nothing, hoping no one agrees or cares that this was just said. (Comfort Zone, Discomfort Zone, Courage Zone)

> **Response 2:** You feel a pit in your stomach as soon as you hear this comment and it's just not sitting right. You don't want to say anything that will start an argument, but you also want

to say something that is supportive of trans people. You feel uncomfortable and are contemplating what to do. (Comfort Zone, Discomfort Zone, Courage Zone)

Response 3: You process the comment in your mind and then thoughtfully reply and say, "I understand that this is your opinion. I imagine it is not easy to live uncomfortably as the incorrect gender or to date someone while being perceived as a gender you do not identify as. Some people are attracted to people as a whole and that includes all of their parts. I think it's cool when someone can be who they are, like who they like, and be liked as the gender and the person they are." (Comfort Zone, Discomfort Zone, Courage Zone)

Scenario 2

You're with two friends after school getting some junk food before going to play video games. Two police officers walk into the store. Your white cisgender friend starts making loud noises and causing a scene while standing next to your Black trans friend who appears to look increasingly uncomfortable.

Response 1: You start to feel nervous butterflies in your stomach because you anticipate something could go very wrong here. You're scared for your trans friend because of her history with law enforcement as a trans person of color in a small community with predominantly white, straight, and cisgender people. You don't want to be silent, but you don't want to pretend you know what it's like to be a trans person of color. (Comfort Zone, Discomfort Zone, Courage Zone)

Response 2: You quickly walk over to your white straight friend making a scene and say, "Hey, you may think it's funny to act this way in front of the police officers but it can be scary for there to be unnecessary attention from the police if you're a person who has been treated unjustly and poorly by law enforcement due to race, gender, sexual orientation, or any other marginalized identity. Please be mindful of this now and next time you are in a situation like this." (Comfort Zone, Discomfort Zone, Courage Zone)

Response 3: Ignore your friends and just continue to grab snacks as quickly as possible to avoid any trouble. (Comfort Zone, Discomfort Zone, Courage Zone)

Scenario 3

You're at a holiday dinner with family. You're sitting at the table with your trans brother and your older cousin in college who is not very understanding of trans experience. Your cousin says to your brother, "Why do you want to make your life harder than it already is? Most people won't accept you for being trans. Do you want to be depressed for the rest of your life?"

Response 1: You start to get that protective vibe and want to throw mashed potatoes at your older cousin, but you don't do it. You feel uneasy but don't want to start something in front of your entire family. (Comfort Zone, Discomfort Zone, Courage Zone)

Response 2: You roll your eyes, ignore your cousin, and try to change the subject to something more positive with your trans brother. (Comfort Zone, Discomfort Zone, Courage Zone)

Response 3: You say softly and confidently to your cousin, "You may be concerned about his safety, but not every trans person has depression or feels that they are making their life harder by being who they are. Many trans people live happy and healthy lives. I am going to do everything I can to support his journey and am inspired by his strength and courage." (Comfort Zone, Discomfort Zone, Courage Zone)

Scenario 1 #1: Comfort; #2: Discomfort; #3: Courage. Scenario 2 #1: Discomfort; #2: Courage; #3: Comfort. Scenario 3 #1: Discomfort; #2 Comfort; #3: Courage.

QUESTIONS ABOUT THE EN/COURAGE ZONE

What are some of the potential barriers for people in the Comfort Zone or Discomfort Zone to get to the Courage Zone?

When a Super Trans Ally is in the Courage Zone, what do you think the impact is on their gender diverse friends and family? Do you think that they feel supported?

How do we start a conversation with others whom we may not know well? One way could be to mention this book! "I'm reading an interesting book about being an ally to my transgender friends and family. I'd love to tell you about it. Would you like to hear more?" See how they respond. Would you be surprised if they shared that they, too, have gender diverse folks in their life? Or that they identify as non-binary? Of course, there is the possibility that they are busy doing their work or that they would not like to engage in such a conversation. But it's worth a try!

Sometimes misgendering happens quickly and requires immediate action. Have a few brief statements on hand for those moments to avoid getting frozen in surprise. One scenario might be that you and your friend and your cousin are going out to the movies.

You buy tickets and walk in. You give your tickets to the ticket taker who makes an assumption about the gender of your group, saying, "Enjoy the show, ladies." Your cousin who is trans masculine does not identify as a lady. You hear the comment, immediately put on your Super Trans Ally cape, and say as you are walking towards the theater, "We're not all ladies."

In advance of such a moment, you may want to have a conversation with your cousin about how they prefer to handle misgendering. Do they want to be the one to make the correction or would they like it if you spoke up? If you do not get to have the conversation with your cousin before an uncomfortable moment happens, it's totally cool to debrief with them after the fact. You can say, "In that moment when the ticket taker misgendered you, was it OK that I spoke up? Would you prefer to make the correction yourself in the future?" Also ask them in general if they prefer to correct people when they use the wrong pronouns or if they are comfortable with you making the correction. How do you correct pronouns? Just use the right pronouns! In the context of the conversation say something like, "My cousin likes movies. He and I saw a great film last week." Or just say, "My cousin uses he/him/his pronouns," and hope the person catches on.

And what if it all goes wrong? Let's say there is no lightbulb going off on top of the person's head, they do not appreciate your efforts, and you are left with no feeling of triumph. What does that mean? Were your efforts wasted? Should you abandon the whole project? Stick to working with animals because humans are so difficult? No way! Yes, animals are great. But humans are worth it. Even when they don't seem to be "getting it" or are actively refusing to participate with you in a learning opportunity, they could still benefit in the future. Think of your efforts as planting seeds. Sure, we'd all love to see our seeds come to fruition and bloom immediately, but not every seed germinates quickly. Some take time and some take lots of time. Maybe in the future the people you were trying to educate will be watching a television show or reading something or having a situation in their own lives that gives them pause. Perhaps something will spark a memory for them of the conversation with you. That seed you planted is now a bud and may bloom soon, or it may take a few more conversations or experiences for them to truly develop the awareness, acceptance, and empathy that you were originally trying to convey to them. So walk away if you must, but trust that your efforts are always worth it. Keep your dignity and continue to have hope for the future.

As a Super Trans Ally, you have already done lots of thinking (and maybe even taken action) regarding making sure your family and friends understand the importance of using correct pronouns and names. Now it's time to fly into action at school. There are many opportunities for ally action with students, teachers, and school district administrators. Oh, my!

SPEAK UP, INTERRUPT, USE HUMOR, DISTRACT

Here are a few tools for your Super Trans Ally toolkit: Speak up, interrupt, use humor, and distract. Let's explore each of these ideas.

Speak up in classroom conversations and assert the rights and dignity of people of all genders. Interrupt people who are gossiping, telling insensitive "jokes," making assumptions, misgendering, or using incorrect names.

Practice the strategy of interrupting by saying quick, simple expressions out loud:

- "Hey!"
- "Wait. What?!?"

- "That's not cool."
- "That's not funny."
- "What's so funny?"
- "What's funny about that?"
- "I don't find that funny."
- "Cut it out."
- "Don't be a hater."
- "Ouch! That hurts."
- "Please stop."
- "That's not a joke."
- "Please don't joke about that."
- "I'm not OK with that."
- "That's insulting."
- "That's disrespectful."
- "Why would you say that?"
- "What's the big deal?"
- "Huh?!?"
- "Are you talking to me?"
- "Why do you think that?"
- "Say, what?"

Circle the expression(s) above that most resonate with you. Practice saying your favorite expressions out loud several times. After you make one or more of those statements to someone, offer to talk about how what was said is hurtful and harmful.

Let's practice interrupting a "joke." Run this role-play with two friends. This scene takes place in a school hallway or lunchroom.

Student 1: Did you see that boy who is wearing makeup?

Student 2: Oh, you mean _____ (birth name)? I've seen better makeup on a clown.

Student 1 and 2: (Laughing.)

You: Hey, that's not cool.

Student 1: What?!? We were just joking. What's the big deal?

You: It's disrespectful.

Student 2: You're too sensitive.

You: I want to tell you how what you said was hurtful.

Student 1: I really don't care. (Walks away.)

Student 2: How was it hurtful? We were just kidding. It's not like we beat the kid up or anything.

You: First, _____ (current name) happens to be someone I care about. Please show respect by using ____ (pronoun: their, her, etc.) current name and pronouns. It's not OK to use incorrect names. Please stop doing that. Second, by making insensitive jokes, you are creating a hostile environment. It's hard to feel like your peers are mocking or judging all the time. Try to put yourself in _____ (name)'s shoes.

Student 2: You sure have a lot to say on the subject.

You: Yes, I do. I'd be happy to talk to you more about it.

Student 2: Maybe another time.

Comments, questions, concerns
This scene could also have taken a path where both students walk

away instead of sticking around to hear how their actions were harmful. Even if that is the case, it's still worth your time to interrupt the original "joke."

Other techniques include using a lighter approach such as saying, "Don't hate her because she's beautiful" or "Don't hate them because they are beautiful." That addresses the pronoun issue, the hate, and gives the person being targeted a compliment (beautiful) all in one short sentence. Cool! While it may not be as direct as speaking explicitly about harm, humor is a useful tool. Another option is to divert the conversation with a fun fact about something that seems unrelated. In this situation it could be a fun fact about clowns. You could also sidetrack the conversation by talking about shoes, the weather, why bees do a waggle dance (look that one up!), or any other favorite off-topic comment of your choice.

If these students are in your friend group and they persist with making insulting comments after you have tried humor and diversion techniques, then it's time to address the concern directly. Where's your Super Trans Ally cape? It's probably best to have a one-on-one conversation with each of the people involved rather than making a blanket statement online or in a group. When people read general statements, they may not necessarily think about their personal actions or responsibility. When people receive feedback in a group, they may get defensive and turn against you. Be thoughtful about taking care of yourself and remember that the people joking or making offensive comments may not realize how they are causing harm. You are educating them and they may or may not appreciate that. Even if your inclination is to be judgmental about their ignorance, try compassion instead.

When it is safe to do so, interrupt bullying using the same

short statements as above. If it is not safe, get help immediately. Sometimes it is worth walking away to collect your thoughts and circling back later with your response to the person being targeted and/or the person or group doing the targeting. Even if some time goes by, it is not too late to express your concern and perspective. Your voice matters. You can be an ally after the incident as well as during. Just having someone say that they saw what happened can often be validating. It also gives the person who was targeted a chance to connect with you and possibly share something really important about their feelings or experience. You can make someone's day or be that lifeline that they have been wishing for.

TEACHING YOUR TEACHERS: CUE SCARY MUSIC—DUN DUN DUN!

You may be thinking, "Who am I to teach my teacher(s)?" Isn't that the job of the school or something my parent(s)/guardian(s) should do? Well, you do have a point there. We would hope that teachers are receiving professional development so that they are well equipped to teach all of their students. Maybe teachers, like other folks, need to hear things a few times to really understand the importance. Generally, teachers care about their students and are willing to listen to suggestions from students provided the feedback is offered in a kind and caring way. Perhaps you could find time before or after class to talk to your teacher in person. Maybe you could ask for a few minutes of the teacher's time before or after school when other students will not be a distraction to you or the teacher.

Some adults may think that young people are there to learn from them and not the other way around. You have a voice. You can flip the switch! Your light is now on! Everyone can be both a teacher and a learner at the same time.

- What do you want to say to your teacher(s)?
- When do you think would be the best time to share your message?
- What support do you need to make this happen?

Like Grandma or your special relative, teachers may hold various personal opinions. We do not want you to get into a debate with a teacher about the gender binary. What matters in this situation is that the teacher understands that their classroom should be a safe and welcoming place for all students and that teacher actions can make a big difference.

If you are hearing transphobic messages from students in a classroom and you are not sure if the teacher heard those statements or saw those gestures or is aware of uncomfortable situations, take time to talk to the teacher privately. If the teacher is not aware of what is going on, they should be informed (in a respectful manner). If they are aware but were not sure how to respond, it's really OK for you to give your perspective on what would be helpful in such a situation and how they might circle back to the issue with the students who were involved. For example, the teacher could talk to the person who was being targeted and let them know they are following up with the offenders. Then the teacher could talk to the offenders or the whole class about respect and how important it is that everyone feels safe and welcome in the classroom and that transphobia or any insensitivity will not be tolerated.

Here are some role-plays for you to practice in preparation for talking to your teacher. It would be good to practice these scenarios with a friend playing the role of the teacher.

Proactive approach at the beginning of the school year or semester (before class or after class or before school or after school) assuming a neutral teacher response

You: Hello, my new teacher. I'm _____ (your name). I'm looking forward to our class together.

Teacher: Hello, _____ (your name).

You: I want to let you know that I care about gender diversity and making our classroom and school as accepting as possible.

Teacher: That's great.

You: I would appreciate it if you would use gender-neutral language for greetings, such as "Welcome, students," "Hello, folks," "Good morning, everyone," or "Good afternoon, friends," instead of "Hello, boys and girls" or "Ladies and gentlemen, please find your seats."

Teacher: Thank you for your request.

You: I'd also like to ask you to not separate the class into "boys and girls." Instead, could we use some other sorting method like even/odd-numbered birthday or number of siblings or first letter of first name in the first half of the alphabet or last half of the alphabet?

Teacher: Creative. I'll give it some thought.

You: Could you please avoid gendered language whenever possible? Instead of calling on us as "young lady" or "young man" or "sir" or "ma'am," could you just use our names (as soon as you learn them)?

Teacher: I can try.

You: I really appreciate your consideration. I am happy to talk more about this subject. Please let me know if you have questions.

Teacher: Thank you.

Notes, questions, concerns

_____

_____

_____

It's always good to be proactive (at the beginning of the school year or beginning of the semester) so that you can later remind the teacher about any concerns. That way, you can avoid the awkward moment of informing the teacher that what they did is hurtful, harmful, or exclusionary as the starting conversation. You can certainly have this conversation with the teacher any time. It doesn't have to be early in the year or semester.

There are two essential parts in the communication with the teacher: (1) asserting yourself as someone who cares about gender diversity and acceptance, and (2) making requests: using gender-neutral language for greetings, separating the class by a method other than the gender binary, and using student names instead of gender markers. Are there any other big ideas that you want to emphasize? Write them here:

1. _____

2. _____

3. _____

It would also be helpful if teachers introduced themselves with their pronouns at the beginning of the school year and if they asked students for their pronouns on a first-day information sheet. Ask the teacher if they can write in or print up class lists with correct names and pronouns (not just print out an official school record with legal names). Before a class/school field trip, ask your teacher to advise the museum, tour guide, or event planner to use gender-neutral/inclusive language rather than gendered language, and avoid calling out people by gender markers such as "the young man in the sparkly sneakers." Ask coaches to print team rosters with correct names and pronouns, and to advise visiting/away coaches and teams to be mindful. We encourage you to make all of these requests of your teacher(s) and coach(es) over time.

What if the teacher's response was less friendly than in the initial scenario? Let's see what it might feel like to role-play an unreceptive teacher response. Know that our intention here is to strengthen your Super Trans Ally tolerance for uncomfortable situations. You can do it!

Unfriendly teacher response

You: Hello, my new teacher. I'm _____ (your name). I'm looking forward to our class together.

Teacher: Hello, _____ (your name).

You: I want to let you know that I care about gender diversity and making our classroom and school as accepting as possible.

Teacher: I treat girls the same way as I treat boys.

You: What I mean is that there may be students in our class who identify as gender non-binary or gender expansive. So, I would appreciate it if you would use gender-neutral language for greetings, such as "Welcome, students," "Hello, folks," "Good morning, everyone," or "Good afternoon, friends," instead of "Hello, boys and girls" or "Ladies and gentlemen, please find your seats."

Teacher: I don't appreciate you telling me how to speak.

You: I'm simply making a request for your consideration so that everyone feels included. I'd also like to ask you not to separate the class into "boys and girls." Instead, could we use some other sorting method like even/odd-numbered birthday or number of siblings or first letter of first name in the first half of the alphabet or last half of the alphabet?

Teacher: There is nothing wrong with separating the class into boys and girls. Everyone is either a boy or a girl. Please take your seat.

You: Thank you for your time.

Notes, questions, concerns

_____

_____

_____

What do you think that teacher's next move would be? Would you expect to get a phone call home from that teacher? Would you expect to be called to the office? If you know a teacher is "old-fashioned," would you consider bringing a friend with you to the conversation for moral support? Are you concerned that the teacher might act differently towards you because of that interaction?

What would your next move be?

In the "unfriendly" role-play, the teacher was direct and

dismissive. What if they were not so direct but their tone or body language revealed their attitude? Could you handle that? Part of what we are developing is the capacity to be comfortable in uncomfortable situations. How do we do that? Practice. And keeping our Super Trans Ally cape on!

BUBBLE GUM: TAKE ACTION

Take it to another level! Just as a proactive approach is helpful with classroom teachers, it is also a good idea to be proactive with the principal and school district administrators such as the superintendent. There are two reasons for this recommendation: first, because you are planting seeds for inclusive policy and practices regarding gender expansive students; second, because you want to have recourse if there is an issue of bullying or no change in an unsupportive classroom dynamic after you have spoken to the teacher.

How does school policy get created and changed? Do you know what school policies apply to students? Do you have a school handbook? Policies would likely be printed there. The policies may also be on the district website. See if you can find any policies related to gender. Do these policies address transgender or gender expansive students? Areas of interest include names and gender markers on official school records, privacy and confidentiality, bathroom and locker-room accessibility, dress code, safety, staff training, preventing harassment and discrimination, and ensuring equity and eliminating stigma. There are model policies online.

If there are no school policies related to transgender or gender expansive students, take your concerns to the principal, superintendent, and school board. What are your ideas about who could help with this project? Are there supportive peers who would be willing to go with you to raise the issue with the principal? Would your parent(s)/guardian(s) be helpful allies and advocates here? Could a group of concerned students and parents raise the issue at a school board meeting? Could a petition calling for inclusive school policy be written and signed by students and parents and delivered to the school board and the news media? Cast as wide a net as possible to harness the collective power of a group of Super Trans Allies for positive change. Include community organizations when possible.

CREATING CHANGE AT SCHOOL

What other ideas do you have about creating change at school? What is needed? What would make a difference?

What if transphobic situations are happening in the school hallways, in the school bathrooms, locker rooms, on the bus, during after-school activities, or on the athletics field? Write down what happened and report all incidents to the principal. One effective means of communicating formally is to write a letter.

LETTER WRITING

When you write a letter or email, share the essential details of the situation or incident. Your voice as a Super Trans Ally makes a difference. You are bringing events to light that may be unrecognized or there may be ongoing efforts. While you may be passionate about the subject, it is best to use professional language. If there are ongoing school efforts around diversity, perhaps those could be used as a springboard. Is there something effective about those efforts or initiatives? Can you frame the concern in such a way that there is a win-win situation? What are the recipient's interests and concerns? Are they concerned about school culture? Positive publicity? Recognition of service? You may find the recipient of the letter more willing to help if they see the possibility of a positive outcome rather than just a complaint.

What are your concerns? Check as many as apply:

- ☐ Insensitive/transphobic language
- ☐ Bullying/harassment/intimidation/violence
- ☐ Being excluded
- ☐ Gendered language or splitting the class/grade into "boys/girls"
- ☐ Name and pronoun issues (e.g. when substitute teacher is taking attendance)
- ☐ School policy
- ☐ Structures such as bathrooms and/or locker rooms
- ☐ School climate
- ☐ Write in: _____
  _____

Where are these events happening? Check as many as apply:

- ☐ In the classrooms
- ☐ In the school hallways
- ☐ In the school bathrooms
- ☐ In locker rooms
- ☐ In the school library
- ☐ On the bus
- ☐ During after-school activities
- ☐ On the athletics field
- ☐ On school grounds

☐ Online/social media

☐ Write in: _____

_____

Who is taking these actions? Check as many as apply:

☐ Students

☐ Teachers

☐ Support staff (teaching aides, secretaries/administrative assistants, security guards)

☐ Guidance counselors, librarians, nurses, or specialists who provide services (reading, speech, hearing, physical/ occupational therapists)

☐ Administrators

☐ Other school personnel (food service professionals, custodians, cleaning staff, volunteers)

☐ Coaches/trainers

☐ Parents of students/community members

☐ Visiting teams/students/coaches

☐ Write in: _____

_____

When are the issues happening? Check as many as apply:

☐ Before school

☐ During class

☐ During lunch

☐ During recess

☐ After school

☐ In the evening

Why are you reaching out to the recipient of the letter? How do you think they can help?

I am reaching out to you because:

What follow-up would you like? Check as many as apply:

- ☐ Meeting to discuss this concern
- ☐ Consequence for students who are bullying or insensitive
- ☐ Assembly for students in a class, grade, or whole school
- ☐ Communication follow-up with teacher
- ☐ Training/professional development for teachers and staff
- ☐ Single-stall bathroom access or locker-room changing accommodation
- ☐ School policy review or new policy

What action/remedy would be the best possible outcome? What would you love to see happen?

I/we would appreciate the opportunity to meet with you to discuss my/our concern and what the school can do to create a more inclusive and accepting culture.

When is this action/remedy needed? Vague time frames like "as soon as possible" mean that your concern could be addressed in five years! Specify a date by which you would like a response to your concern. For example:

> I would appreciate receiving your response to this letter by: _____ (date).
>
> Please reply to _____ (your name if there are multiple people who signed) via _____ (specify email address or other options such as being called to the office).
>
> Thank you for your time and consideration.
>
> Sincerely,
>
> (Name(s))

When you send this letter and perhaps have a follow-up meeting, it is helpful to remember that the recipient is probably busy. Unless you know where they stand, assume they know little or nothing about gender expansive concerns. Where is your Super Trans Ally cape? Get ready to do some quick basic education about gender diversity! Presume goodwill—that is, that they want to help if they can—and that they likely feel their hands are tied by structures that already exist such as bathrooms and that there is little to no money available for changes. How can you proceed? Remember to stay calm. We don't want the recipient to get defensive and stop listening or resist helping. We want to enlist their creative problem-solving capacity. When they say something like "We can't very well build a new bathroom—there's no money in the budget for that and it would take years to get approved," you can suggest using the nurse's bathroom or a single-stall bathroom in the office. Keep offering potential solutions from a different perspective. Keep inviting them to be your ally and help figure out how to make the school an accepting, more inclusive, and safer place for all students. That is their job.

SELF-CHECK-IN ABOUT LETTER WRITING

- How do you feel about this letter?
- Are you concerned that there might be consequences?
- What would those consequences be?
- Are there other students who share your concerns? Would they be willing to sign their names as well?

Give yourself some recognition for writing the letter! Add this to the Super Trans Ally action chart in Chapter 9. Whatever the outcome of the letter, know that you are using your voice and power in important ways. Thank you for your service!

Follow-up letter

Always take time to thank the recipient of the letter for their time and consideration. Even if the outcome is not what you would consider positive, keep the conversation going and flowing by sending a thank-you note. It can be handwritten or sent by email. Here is the essence: "Thank you for reading my letter and taking the time to meet with me. I am grateful that you are taking action to create a more accepting school culture. I appreciate your partnership in this urgent endeavor. Please let me know how I can be supportive."

How are you feeling about your Super Trans Ally mission to "school everyone"? Write a few notes to yourself about your feelings or next action steps:

_____

_____

_____

SCHOOL VISIBILITY

Here are a few additional thoughts about requests you could make for school visibility:

- Recommend books to your school library. Talk to the librarian about creating a featured display of LGBTQIAPNBGD+ books. Emphasize the need for books about gender identity and gender expression.
- Ask the school guidance department, teachers, and administrators to display LGBTQIAPNBGD+-affirming posters in their offices and classrooms. Emphasize the need for posters featuring diverse gender identity and gender expression.
- Request a hallway display case or bulletin board to create and feature terms and concepts related to gender and how to be respectful of people's names and pronouns. Highlight a few key ally actions and include bold visuals so people walking by quickly get an impression.
- Request a guest speaker for the class/grade/school or an assembly for education around gender diverse inclusivity.
- Host a Rainbow Dance at which people of all genders (including allies) are welcome.

Do you have other great ideas about how to "school everyone"? Who else needs to hear from you? Note the names and ideas here:

Ideas:

Name(s) and issue(s):

We are so excited for you to start or continue educating others. You are going to be one of those great teachers we think of fondly!

CHAPTER 9

Be a Super Trans Ally and Change the World!

What does it mean to change the world? How does change happen? What if the world is not changing fast enough for you? How can we turn frustration into action? How can we care deeply for our gender diverse friends and family and take good care of ourselves? What does it mean to be a lifelong learner? What does it mean to be a committed Super Trans Ally?

Ally Action is super cool! Do you agree? It can be rewarding and exciting to take Super Trans Ally action. Sometimes it may be a little tense, and it takes time to develop confidence and comfort with this skill. Please do not be hard on yourself if you are not comfortable speaking up or taking a stand in every situation. Always assess safety in the moment. Sometimes it might be best to get help or follow-up with someone who is being targeted after the fact if there is potential danger. If, on the other hand, the situation is uncomfortable and not dangerous and you just feel stuck, resolve to practice speaking up and do more next time.

What are you motivated to do?

As you read through the list, put an asterisk (*) or star next to any item which you would consider doing. Put a check mark (✓) next to actions that you do on a regular basis and plan to continue in the future.

SUPER TRANS ALLY CHECKLIST

- ☐ Introduce yourself with your name and pronouns.
- ☐ Ask people their name and pronouns.
- ☐ Be proactive about remembering and using correct names and pronouns.
- ☐ Correct your own errors with name or pronouns.
- ☐ Correct others when they misgender someone (in front of the person or when referencing the person).
- ☐ Educate yourself (yes, reading this book counts!).
- ☐ Educate others.
- ☐ Offer others suggestions for where to find resources created by people with lived gender diverse experiences (videos, books, groups, conferences).
- ☐ Brainstorm with peers about what creative actions you can take as a group.
- ☐ Organize an event where trans people are featured presenters.
- ☐ Host a (dance) party for gender diverse folks and allies.
- ☐ Hold a fashion show.
- ☐ Support gender expansive youth art and business.
- ☐ Plan a school or community dinner as a fundraiser for trans organizations.
- ☐ Talk to your teacher(s) about trans and non-binary acceptance and inclusion.
- ☐ Gather a group of allies together to brainstorm with school administrators (principal, vice principal, deans) about creating

and sustaining a fully accepting and inclusive school culture. This can be done with or without funding. For example, create a visual display about trans acceptance with photos of allies and resources; make a presentation to the teachers and staff at your school with a gender expansive friend to help teachers and staff understand what actions they can take to support trans and non-binary students in classrooms, hallways, bathrooms and locker rooms, the lunchroom, the gym, through curriculum across all subject areas, and through sporting and school-based social events.

☐ Encourage best-practice school policies: ensure that current names and pronouns are notated on the class list for the classroom teacher and substitute teacher. Ask your teacher or coach if they can write in or print up class lists or team rosters with correct names and pronouns (not just print out an official school record with legal names).

☐ Report issues of concern to the school administration or have your parent(s)/guardian(s) do so.

☐ Speak with your school guidance counselor about your concerns, hopes, and dreams.

☐ Work with the school curriculum director, principal, or school board to ensure that trans bodies, experiences, sexual health, and relationships are included in the general health class.

☐ Personal visibility: wear a T-shirt, put a bumper sticker on your car, put a lawn sign in front of your house, wear a button on your school bag, post a symbol on your social media—let people know you are there for them.

☐ Recommend books to your school library (mentioned in Chapter 8). Talk to the librarian about creating a featured display of LGBTQIAPNBGD+ books. Emphasize the need for books about gender identity and gender expression.

☐ Promote school visibility (mentioned in Chapter 8). Ask the school guidance department, teachers, and administrators to display posters that affirm LGBTQIAPNBGD+ students in their offices and classrooms. Emphasize the need for posters featuring gender identity and gender expression.

☐ "I'll go with you." Talk to teachers in advance about accompanying your gender diverse classmate to the bathroom or locker room. What arrangements are there for gender-neutral bathrooms and locker rooms?

☐ Talk to your gender diverse friends about what support they need on school transportation or public transportation.

☐ Talk to your parent(s)/guardian(s) or trusted adult allies about getting the support *you* need.

☐ Speak up in class discussions.

☐ Create and/or sustain an ally action group.

☐ Hold an open-mic event for gender diverse performance artists and allies.

☐ Write a news article or comic about trans issues for your school paper.

☐ Write a poem or short story featuring a gender expansive character for your school's literary magazine.

☐ Write a letter to a local newspaper.

☐ Gather a few Super Trans Allies (students and parents) together to bring issues of school district policy to the school board.

☐ Contact your region's elected officials regarding transgender rights and inclusive policies.

☐ Regularly attend your school's gender and sexuality alliance meetings. If such a club does not already exist, start one.

☐ Interrupt people who are gossiping, telling insensitive "jokes," making assumptions, misgendering, or using incorrect names.

Practice using quick, simple expressions like "Hey!" or "That's not cool!" or "Ouch! That hurts." Offer to talk about how what was said is hurtful/harmful.

☐ Interrupt bullying or bias incidents.

☐ Delegate to a trusted adult to get involved if you believe something should be done and you need help addressing a situation (i.e. bullying or bias incident).

☐ Use inclusive language—"we" rather than us/them.

☐ Create your own artistic expression of what being a Super Trans Ally means to you (dance, song, poetry, story, video, sewing, drawing, collage, other art, writing a book, creating a video game, etc.).

☐ Perform or showcase your creation that expresses what it means to be an ally or educate about acceptance and inclusion of all genders. Hold a coffeehouse or open-mic poetry slam.

☐ Write a play.

☐ Gather a group of friends and/or family together to watch and discuss a movie about trans people's lives or social issues related to trans experiences.

☐ Create a Super Trans Ally Squad. Insulate/buffer/protect your trans friends and family by traveling together in a supportive group. This makes it easier to deflect and process any bullying that might occur. Report any and all incidents, no matter how slight.

☐ Write a loving and affirming note to your trans loved one or express your support another way.

☐ Talk to a trusted adult if you have concerns about your gender expansive friend or family member's mental health.

☐ Reward yourself for your Super Trans Ally actions (see the gold star section and rewards section later in this chapter).

☐ What else? What excites you and offers you an opportunity to create space for your trans friends and family? Write that in:

ACTION ITEMS FROM THE SUPER TRANS ALLY CHECKLIST

Review the Super Trans Ally checklist and record which new items (notated with an asterisk *) you intend to take action on. Note whether these are immediate, near-future, or long-term actions. For long-term action items, consider a best possible date to start. If there are items that you already do routinely, only add them to the list if there is a new twist to your efforts.

Super Trans Ally action I will take	Immediate or near future	Start date if long-term

Are you excited and motivated to make things happen? Here's a template to help you organize your ideas in one place.

TEMPLATE FOR PLANNING AN EVENT FOR TRANS FOLKS AND ALLIES

- What kind of event is this? Are trans and non-binary folks at the center?
- Who will be featured?
- Who is the intended audience?
- When will be the best date and time for this event?
- Where will the event be held?
- Why are you organizing this event? What is your intention?
- Are trans and non-binary folks involved in planning and organizing?
- Whose help will you enlist?
- Do you need permission?
- How will you access the space?
- Is it wheelchair accessible?
- Will there be a sign language interpreter?
- Is there a rental fee for the space?
- Will you collect money at the door for tickets?
- How will you secure the money?
- Will some or all of the money be donated?
- How will you (or the organizing committee) decide which trans organization will be the recipient of the donation?
- Will you need a paid security guard or will adult volunteers be sufficient?
- Who will organize and train the volunteers?

- How will you advertise the event?
- Will food be served?
- Who will handle the food arrangements?
- Who will arrive early to set up and decorate and/or clean up at the end of the event?

Regardless of the turn-out for the event, reward yourself for organizing! This is a great life experience and we hope that you have fun in the process. This is what community-building is all about. We may never really know whose life is positively impacted by our efforts. Trust in your heart that someone or many people will benefit, even if there are challenges along the way.

Write about your organizing efforts and experiences below. Keep the focus on your Super Trans Ally action and "look with love" at your efforts rather than criticizing yourself. If something did not go as you had hoped or planned, learn from the experience and resolve to do it differently in the future.

RECOGNIZING MY SUPER TRANS ALLY ACHIEVEMENT(S)

On _____ (date), I took Super Trans Ally action when I (describe what you did): _____

_____

_____

_____

Helper/support people: _____

_____

_____

_____

Outcome of the action: _____

_____

_____

_____

How I felt: _____

_____

_____

_____

What worked? What would I change in the future?

_____

_____

_____

How will I reward or recognize myself for this action?

_____

_____

WHAT WOULD BE A FUN WAY TO REWARD OR RECOGNIZE YOURSELF?

Ideas bank: Circle items that interest you.

Create art (draw, paint, collage, color, work with clay, make crafts, take photographs, work with wood, make jewelry, graphic design, interior design, fashion design, etc.)

dance

sing

listen to or make music

read a book

write

give yourself a sticker

create a card or award for yourself

play a game

take a walk or run

ride a bike

play sports

stretch or do yoga

connect with a friend or Super Trans Ally buddy

play with a toy

play with an animal

connect with nature

hold a crystal

play dress up

style your hair

laugh out loud

enjoy a healthy treat

sip some tea or cocoa

cook or bake something

sew/knit/crochet

watch a favorite movie or show

cozy up with a blanket

watch the sunrise or sunset

take a bath/shower or swim

breathe mindfully or meditate

plant something or tend a garden

go to your favorite place

daydream

create a box with kind words or affirmations for yourself and pick one (and say the affirmation out loud several times to yourself)

go to a museum or library

look lovingly into your own eyes and say how proud you are of yourself

learn something new

enjoy a favorite or new pastime

organize something

set a little money in a jar to save for a bigger reward

What else can you think of that would bring you joy? Write in:

Write in your favorite ways to reward or recognize yourself:

1. --

2. --

3. --

GOLD STAR/SHARE IT FORWARD

It is delightful and nourishing to recognize our own actions and it can be heartwarming to recognize the efforts of others. We also love the action of accentuating the positive because it is often so easy to criticize ourselves or others. Can we remember to say positive things to ourselves and others? We can consciously develop this skill and habit. Can we refrain from gossip and hurtful comments? Can we nurture positive self-talk? Can we assume that people are doing the best they can? Can we notice what is going well? Can we verbalize what is going well? Can we give constructive feedback that recognizes the good rather than just criticism? We can and must appreciate our own efforts and focus on the good in others. This alone is an amazing action, which is free and can make a huge difference!

What is a "gold star"? Does the idea of being appreciated and recognized appeal to you? Many people respond positively to kind words whether they show it or not. Sometimes people may seem to brush off or dismiss a compliment. Perhaps they are not used to receiving praise, recognition or appreciation. Perhaps they do not see their actions as significant. Perhaps they struggle with self-esteem. Even if they do not receive your "gold star" with excitement, give it anyway. A "gold star" can be a sticker, a note, a smile, a verbal "pat on the back," a kind word, a recognition of effort, heartfelt appreciation, or any other gesture of recognition. Most importantly, offer the "gold star" with love and kindness.

Pass a "gold star" to a person who took a Super Trans Ally action and tell them how their action(s) inspired you, impressed you, or made a difference. The "share it forward" aspect is to ask the recipient of the star to tell another person (family/friend/ally) something they notice and appreciate.

Record one Gold Star Recognition:

On _____ (date), I noticed _____ (name) took Super Trans Ally action by (describe the action):

I recognized their Super Trans Ally action by (describe what you did and said):

They responded by:

INSPIRED? READY FOR ACTION?
· ·

How are you feeling about being a Super Trans Ally?

☐ I am excited for the journey.

If you are excited, we are excited! Yay!

☐ I feel overwhelmed because I am just one person.

Yes, you are one person. Remember that you are one among many people who care deeply for our gender expansive friends and relatives. You are not alone as a Super Trans Ally. We are with you! Every action you take resonates and builds momentum. Remind yourself, "I can do this! It's a choice and I can make a difference!"

☐   I need more resources.

Be sure to check out the resources section at the end of this guide. There are also many useful resources online and in many communities. Search for keywords like "ally to transgender people" or "ally action." Join forces with others who are working to make their homes, schools, and communities safer and more inclusive for people of all genders. Super Trans Ally action is often free and everyone can participate.

We love the image of the Super Trans Allies in their windswept capes. Throughout this book, we have encouraged you to put on a Super Trans Ally cape to represent having courage and taking action. Can you visualize the cape even when you are not wearing an actual piece of cloth? Visualize your cape whenever you need to be reminded that you always have the power to be a Super Trans Ally.

CHART TO RECORD YOUR SUPER TRANS ALLY ACTIONS

Use the chart below or devote a journal to recording your Super Trans Ally actions. That way you will see an accumulation of your efforts and results. It can be motivational to look back on actions that may have been forgotten. A journal is also a great place to record what worked and what you might do differently. Remember to record in writing what you did to reward and recognize yourself. If you have taken Super Trans Ally actions prior to reading this book, record those items as well.

Date	Star or self-reward ★	Super Trans Ally action description	Notes and reflections

DREAMING THE WORLD TO COME

What is your vision for the world? Do you dare to let yourself dream? Are you so focused on daily life that it's hard to imagine a different future? Let's try a brief experiment. This is something that can be done anywhere at any time. OK, well, be cautious while you are walking somewhere or driving. Read through these steps and then give it a try. See what comes to you.

1. Sit or lie comfortably.

2. Close your eyes.

3. How does the air in the room or outdoors feel to you? Notice the temperature and air quality.

4. Pay attention to your breathing. Notice whether you are breathing deeply or shallowly or if your breath gets stuck anywhere.

5. Feel the energy in your heart. Can you feel your heartbeat? It's OK if not. Just go with whatever you feel.

6. Appreciate your heart. Give gratitude for its rhythm.

7. Keep breathing deeply. Ask your heart for wisdom and a vision for the world.

YOUR VISION FOR AN INCLUSIVE WORLD

What did your heart say? Record any notes about your vision for an inclusive world:

_____

_____

_____

_____

_____

_____

_____

_____

_____

_____

_____

Continue to hold on to your vision. Draw or paint a picture of what you saw. Write a poem, story, or song about the feeling of total acceptance. Your vision and our collective visions help bring this dream into reality.

We envision a day when this book will no longer be needed; when there is acceptance for all human diversity. There is room for all of us. We can find our way together with love and devotion, mutual respect, interconnection, and care for the Earth. You are part of this dream we have. You are part of the solution. Your action is essential. Until the day this book is no longer needed, be a Super Trans Ally all of the time so that gender diverse folks and people of all diversities do not have to shoulder the burden alone. Use all of the tools that you have in your tool kit to interrupt any insensitivity and build structures of inclusion across race, nationality, ethnicity, age, social class, religion, gender identity, gender expression, sexual orientation, disability, neurodiversity, mental health status, family configuration, immigration status, educational level, and more. Keep using your voice, brain, heart, and body to make the world a better place. Continually affirm your choice to take ally action. It makes a difference. We are so grateful and proud to call you a Super Trans Ally. Thank you for your devotion and service. The world needs you.

You finished reading this book and completing the activities! Write that in on the Super Trans Ally action chart and give yourself a star! Congratulations! Keep learning. Keep taking Super Trans Ally action. We are cheering you on!

Glossary of Terms

Note: The definitions for the terms below do not apply to everyone who identifies as and/or experiences them. These terms are always evolving and there is not a singular or complete way to define any particular sexual or gender identity. While it is always appropriate to use the terms for yourself and to describe your own experience, some people may find some of the terms below offensive. No one can label or define any part of another person's identity for them. Only the person can tell us how they self-identify and what their experience means to them. Some people do not choose to label themself regardless of how they experience their gender identity, expression, and/or sexual orientation. The definitions in the box are the framework for the other definitions throughout the glossary.

> **Gender identity**   A person's internal perception or knowledge of their gender as a woman, man, a mix of both, neither, or another gender entirely.

Gender expression   How a person expresses their gender on the outside, including clothing, hair, behavior, or body characteristics. A person's expression does not imply their gender.

Sexual orientation   A person's physical, emotional, romantic, and/or sexual attraction to another person. A person may experience attraction on some or all of these levels. Sexual and romantic attraction can be separate from each other.

Sex   Is assigned as male or female (or intersex) at birth, and based on a combination of chromosomes, hormones, internal and external reproductive organs, and secondary sex characteristics.

LGBTQ+   An acronym and umbrella term for lesbian, gay, bisexual, transgender, and queer/questioning. The "+" encompasses all sexual orientations and gender identities.

LGBTQIAPNBGD+   Another acronym and variation of an umbrella term for lesbian, gay, bisexual, transgender, queer, intersex, asexual, pansexual, non-binary, and gender diverse. Any person can use whatever acronym and variation of the umbrella to reflect what feels most inclusive to and for them. The authors use the acronym LGBTQIAPNBGD+ throughout the book to reflect the infinite sexual orientations and gender identities that exist today, tomorrow, and beyond.

Agender   A person who does not have a gender. Some people may also identify as gender neutrois, gender neutral, or genderless.

Allosexual   A person who does experience sexual attraction. A term used to describe someone who is not asexual.

Androgyne   A person who does not fit exclusively into stereotypical masculine and feminine gender roles. Some people use the term androgynous. Some people who are androgyne identify as non-binary or genderqueer.

Androsexual   A person who is primarily sexually, romantically, and/or emotionally attracted to masculinity.

Aromantic (aro)   A person who has little or no romantic attraction to others.

Asexual (ace)   A person who has little or no sexual attraction to others. Some asexual people experience romantic attraction. Asexuality exists on a continuum.

Bigender   A person who may experience their gender sometimes as only boy/man or girl/woman, sometimes as boy/man and girl/woman, or sometimes as two other genders that may include a gender other than boy/man or girl/woman.

Bisexual   A person who can experience attraction to more than one gender. May be used interchangeably with pansexual depending on what it means to the person experiencing it.

Butch   A person of any gender who presents with what are considered masculine traits. Other terms which indicate butch identities in Black/ African American communities include stud, boi or aggressive (AG).

Ceterosexual   A person who is non-binary and experiences sexual and/ or romantic attraction only to non-binary people. Some people identify as gay and non-binary.

Cisgender (cis)   A person whose gender is the same gender as they were thought to be when they were born (some refer to this as gender assigned at birth). A term used to describe people who are not trans.

Demiromantic   A person who may experience romantic attraction after developing an emotional connection.

Demisexual   A person with little or no sexual attraction until they feel a strong romantic connection with someone.

Female Assigned at Birth (FAAB) or Male Assigned at Birth (MAAB) These terms are generally used to denote what sex was put on someone's birth certificate. This is preferred language to biological sex or born as male/female. Assigned sex at birth is separate from a person's gender identity and gender expression. The terms FAAB and MAAB can be used in an intrusive way which can be offensive.

Femme   A person of any gender who presents with what are considered feminine traits.

Finsexual   A person with an attraction to femininity.

Gay   A person who is attracted only or primarily to people of the same gender. Often used to refer to men/boys who are attracted to other men/boys, and women/girls who are attracted to other women/girls. A person can be gay and cisgender or gay and trans or gay and non-binary.

Gender affirmation   Some people view their coming out as an affirmation of the gender they have always been, rather than a transition from one gender to another. They may use the language "affirmed female" or just "female" or "affirmed male" or just "male." Some people do not feel that "trans" describes their experience since it suggests that they have changed genders.

Gender diverse   An umbrella term for people whose gender identity and/or expression do not conform to societal norms and expectations.

Gender dysphoria   Some people use this term to describe an experience of discomfort related to a mismatch between their gender identity, gender expression, and their gender assigned at birth. Not all trans and non-binary people experience or label their experience gender dysphoria. Gender dysphoria is not a prerequisite for transitioning. Being transgender or non-binary is not a disorder.

Gender euphoria   Describes an intense feeling of happiness and excitement about one's body and identity. The feeling may be associated with self-acceptance and/or feeling that one's gender is affirmed. A person may experience gender dysphoria or gender euphoria, both at the same time or at different times, or neither dysphoria nor euphoria.

Gender fluid   A person who may experience their gender as a mix of boy/man and girl/woman, and may also fluctuate between feeling more like a boy/man or a girl/woman. A person can also be fluid between binary and non-binary gender(s).

Gender nonconforming (GNC)   A person whose gender expression is different from traditional societal expectations of masculinity and femininity. Some people who identify outside of the gender binary identify as GNC. Being GNC is not the same as being trans.

Genderqueer   A person who may not identify as exclusively boy/man or girl/woman (can be both a boy/man and a girl/woman at the same time or neither).

Gender transition   A period of time during which a person begins to live as the gender they are. Transition may or may not include changes in a person's name, pronouns, appearance, voice, or how they dress. Some people change their legal documentation and some people change physical characteristics through hormone therapy or other medical procedures. A transition may occur over a period of time. Some people find the term offensive and prefer terms including gender affirmation or process of gender affirmation.

Gynosexual   A person who is primarily sexually, romantically, and/or emotionally attracted to femininity.

Grey-romantic   A person with a romantic orientation somewhere between aromantic and romantic.

Intersex   An umbrella term that describes a person whose genetic, hormonal, or anatomical combination differs from patterns of the male and female binary. Intersex people may identify as LGBTQIAPNBGD+, straight, cisgender, or any other sexual orientation and gender.

Lesbian   A girl/woman who is primarily attracted to other girls/women.

Mx. (pronounced mix)   An honorific (i.e. Mr., Ms., Mrs., Mx.) that is gender neutral. Some trans, non-binary and other folx who identify outside of a gender binary opt to use Mx (folx is the all-gender inclusive way to spell folks).

Non-binary   A person who identifies beyond the existing social definitions of two genders. They may not identify exclusively as male/boy/man or female/girl/woman. They may feel that they are both male/boy/man and female/girl/woman or neither. They may feel that they fall somewhere in between male/boy/man and female/girl/woman or a different gender or not define their gender.

Panromantic   a person who can be romantically attracted to people of all genders.

Pansexual (pan)   A person who is physically, emotionally, and/or romantically attracted to people of all gender identities and expressions. Some would describe it as an attraction that disregards gender.

Polyamorous   A person who may have the desire for and/or be in an intimate relationship with more than one partner, with the consent of all partners they are involved with.

Polygender   A person who identifies as more than one gender and includes only genders of the person's culture.

Pomosexuality   A descriptor for people who do not use labels to describe their sexuality and who challenge assumptions about sexuality and gender.

Queer   An umbrella term to describe people who do not identify as straight and/or cisgender. In the past, this word was used to put down LGBTQIAPNBGD+ people. Today the word queer can be used in a positive way within LGBTQIAPNBGD+ communities and may be used interchangeably with LGBTQIAPNBGD+. Queer can also indicate radical acceptance and/or a rejection of racism, sexism, sizeism, ableism, and other forms of oppression that are often evident in mainstream LGBTQIAPNBGD+ communities.

Questioning   A person who may be unsure about or exploring their sexual orientation and/or gender identity.

Sapiosexual   A person who is primarily attracted to a person's intelligence.

Skoliosexual   A person who is primarily attracted to transgender and/or non-binary people.

Third gender   A person who does not identify as boy/man or girl/woman, and who identifies as another gender.

Transgender/trans   Can be used to describe a person whose gender identity is different from the gender they were thought to be when they were born.

Trans boy/man/guy   A boy/man/guy who was assigned female at birth and transitioned (socially, medically, and/or legally) to their gender identity. Some people prefer to keep trans in their identity, while others do not include trans in their identity and some do not identify as trans.

Transsexual   An older term that originated in the medical and psychological communities. It is not an umbrella term. Most trans people prefer the word *transgender/trans*. Some folks who are from older generations self-identify as transsexual.

Trans girl/woman   A girl/woman who was assigned male at birth and transitioned (socially, medically, and/or legally) to their gender identity. Some prefer to keep trans in their identity, while others do not include trans in their identity and some do not identify as trans.

Two Spirit   A modern unifying term for Indigenous LGBTQIAPNBGD+ people. Historically, many indigenous nations/tribes have their own terms for people who participated in traditionally masculine and feminine ceremonial or cultural roles.

Resources

There are hundreds of educational and advocacy resources for supporting trans, non-binary, and gender expansive youth. The resources below will also have links to even more great resources!

Gender Spectrum (support and education)
www.genderspectrum.org

Trans Student Educational Resources (TSER) (advocacy for changes in school policy)
http://transstudent.org

TrevorSpace (social networking for LGBTQ+ and allied youth)
www.trevorspace.org

Trans Lifeline (trans-led support hotline for trans communities) (877-565-8860 USA; 877-330-6366 Canada)
www.translifeline.org

The Trevor Project Lifeline (USA suicide prevention lifeline, chat/text, and programming) (1-866-488-7386 USA)
www.thetrevorproject.org

National Center for Transgender Equality (NCTE) (advocacy)
http://transequality.org

GLSEN (education and advocacy)
www.glsen.org

Transgender Law Center (TLC) (legal services and advocacy)
http://transgenderlawcenter.org

Trans People of Color Coalition (TPOCC) (advocacy)
https://transpoc.org

Trans Women of Color Collective (TWOCC) (advocacy)
www.twocc.us

Black Trans Advocacy (advocacy)
https://btac.blacktrans.org

Trans Latina Coalition (advocacy)
www.translatinacoalition.org

Gender Diversity (support for families, trans youth, and educators)
www.genderdiversity.org

Trans Youth Equality Federation (support for families and trans youth)
www.transyouthequality.org

Trans Youth Family Allies (TYFA) (support for families and trans youth)
www.imatyfa.org

TransAthlete.com (info about trans athletes)
www.transathlete.com

Philadelphia Trans Wellness Conference (national conference)
www.mazzonicenter.org/trans-wellness

GLAAD's Transgender Media Program (media advocacy)
http://glaad.org/transgender

PFLAG's Transgender Ally campaign (advocacy)
www.straightforequality.org/trans

Human Rights Campaign: Transgender Resources (education and advocacy)
https://hrc.org/explore/topic/transgender-children-youth

TransJustice at the Audre Lorde Project (advocacy)
http://alp.org/TransJustice

I AM: Trans People Speak (campaign)
http://community.transpeoplespeak.org

The Transgender Training Institute, Inc. (training, consulting, classes)
www.transgendertraininginstitute.com

About the Authors

Phoenix and Sherry are chosen family to each other. We both delighted in the synergy of writing this book together. We collaborate to present diversity sessions for youth, educators, and community. We look forward to connecting with Super Trans Allies!

Phoenix Schneider, MSW (he/him/his/Phoenix) is a trans queer author, trainer, and inclusion coach from Philadelphia. Phoenix's home is always where the heart is, with his family, and he currently lives in Phoenix, AZ, with his partner, Jess, and their three fur-babies, Punky, Jack, and Cleo.

Nearly 20 years ago, Phoenix crossed paths with a group of teens in a local park who were kicked out of their homes for being LGBTQIAPNBGD+. Phoenix brought them back to his small studio apartment to provide shelter and food for the night. That experience was heartbreaking, but it inspired him to pursue more meaningful work to support and empower LGBTQIAPNBGD+ communities. Phoenix's career journey has included work with LGBTQIAPNBGD+ communities throughout the country, including with PFLAG national in D.C., the NYC LGBT Center, and The Trevor Project as the Program Director overseeing suicide prevention programming for LGBTQIAPN-BGD+ youth nationwide. He founded Coach Phoenix Consulting in 2013 and specializes in providing inclusion coaching, and training to schools, nonprofits, corporations, and other institutions throughout the country (www.coachphoenix.com). Phoenix is the author of the children's picture book *Pink, Blue, & All the SHADES of You!* This book encourages young children to be themselves and to express their gender in the ways that make them feel happy.

Phoenix received his Master of Social Work degree from Hunter College School of Social Work. He considers himself to be a teacher and a student for life. He is committed to supporting, educating, and empowering LGBTQIAPNBGD+ and allied young people to cultivate compassion, advocate for their peers, and become agents of change in their communities. All of the young people that Phoenix has had the honor of meeting and working together with over the years have inspired him to continue on his lifelong mission to promote culture shifts toward, full acceptance and inclusion for everyone.

Sherry Paris, MEd (she/her/hers) is a gay/queer cisgender woman who lives in Philadelphia with her beloved life partner, Mel. She is an author, illustrator, and diversity trainer who was named the National Liberty Museum's first "Teacher as Superhero" in 2017. Sherry is on a mission to co-create a world in which everyone is respected, included, accepted, and appreciated for who they truly are. She combines a passion for social justice with her love of education to write as well as design and lead interactive sensitivity training for students, educators, industry leaders, and community. Ms. Paris (her teacher name!) proudly collaborated with young people for 20 years to create a safe and welcoming school district through her leadership of a high-school-based diversity training program. Sherry activates youth allies through education and empowerment, creating spaces where high school students lead activities and conversations about diversity issues with middle school students and with each other. Sherry hosted meetings and an annual diversity conference for high school students to listen and learn from those with lived experience, to create conversations about diversity and social justice, to accept and stand up for themselves and others using allyship strategies and to use their voices to interrupt bias incidents and educate others.

Sherry holds a Master's degree in the Science of Instruction from Drexel University and taught high school mathematics for 22 years.